EXPERT WITNESS

Also by Ann Wolbert Burgess and
Steven Matthew Constantine:

*A Killer by Design: Murderers, Mindhunters,
and My Quest to Decipher the Criminal Mind*

EXPERT WITNESS

THE WEIGHT
OF OUR TESTIMONY
WHEN JUSTICE HANGS
IN THE BALANCE

ANN WOLBERT BURGESS
and
STEVEN MATTHEW CONSTANTINE

GRAND
CENTRAL

New York Boston

Grand Central Publishing
Hachette Book Group
1290 Avenue of the Americas, New York, NY 10104
grandcentralpublishing.com
@grandcentralpub

First Edition: September 2025

Grand Central Publishing is a division of Hachette Book Group, Inc. The Grand Central Publishing name and logo is a registered trademark of Hachette Book Group, Inc.

The publisher is not responsible for websites (or their content) that are not owned by the publisher.

The Hachette Speakers Bureau provides a wide range of authors for speaking events. To find out more, go to hachettespeakersbureau.com or email HachetteSpeakers@hbgusa.com.

Grand Central Publishing books may be purchased in bulk for business, educational, or promotional use. For information, please contact your local bookseller or the Hachette Book Group Special Markets Department at special.markets@hbgusa.com.

Library of Congress Control Number: 2025935087

ISBNs: 978-0-3068-3404-2 (hardcover), 978-0-3068-3406-6 (ebook)

Printed in the United States of America

LSC-H

Printing 1, 2025

To the victims, to the survivors, to the ones we lost,
and to those who feel stuck somewhere in between

Contents

Author's Note

The conversations in this book come from transcriptions and recordings of true events as they actually happened. However, in instances when records were unavailable, I've conveyed conversations based on contextual documentation and the best of my memory.

EXPERT WITNESS

The Rise of the Expert Witness

There's nothing more absolute than a courtroom. It's the biggest stage for the biggest cases with the highest stakes. Sometimes it's a matter of life or death. Sometimes it's the prospect of a multi-billion-dollar payout for victims of corporate malpractice. And sometimes its meaning goes far beyond anything money can touch, like remorse, dignity, repentance, and the terrible burden of being put on display for the entire world to see. But whatever the circumstances, the purpose of a trial always comes down to the same two things: truth and justice. It's as simple as that.

Vincit omnia veritas.
The truth conquers all things.

As an expert witness, I've learned to hold that phrase as a personal mantra. It helps me block out distractions and focus on my one singular goal: to stand before a jury of twelve people and explain, in precise, calm clarity, why a certain gunshot pattern means what it means, or how the neurobiology of trauma can cause a witness to remember the exact geometric pattern of subway tiles but not the face of the man who raped her. I've done this as a court-recognized expert on mental illness, rape, violence, posttraumatic stress disorder, crime classification, profiling, the neurobiology of trauma, elder abuse, infant and child abduction, and countless other specialized topics. I've testified as an expert on nationally televised cases that millions of people tuned in for, and I've worked behind closed doors on cases no one's ever heard about. I've helped legal teams devise strategy. I've squared off against lawyers chomping at the bit to undermine my credibility. I've seen the faces of victims contort into something far beyond grief.

And through it all, I've learned to hold pain at arm's length. Not because I don't feel it—I do, acutely—but because to rise to that witness stand with my integrity intact, I must set aside my own feelings, my personal politics, my instincts to comfort or to rage. I must remember my job. Because, ultimately, the jury, those twelve ordinary people plucked from their lives, are the ones who hold the potential to shift the course of someone's entire existence. My task is to focus solely on what I can control, to speak the truth to the best of my ability.

It's a complicated thing, being an expert witness. Courtrooms are hostile places where words become swords. Despite the specific nature of each case and the individuals involved, it's rarely just individuals who are on trial. Instead, trials tend to be about something messier, something more amorphous, more manipulable—like memory, or trauma, or the way prevailing cultural expectations can either illuminate or completely distort the reality of events.

And so that's the challenge. Every time I walk into that courtroom, I pass rows and rows of scuffed benches and nervous relatives, I hear the click, click, click of the stenographer's keys, and I make my way to the witness box, right next to the judge. From the second I enter the arena, I know that every syllable, every hesitation, every minor adjustment of my glasses or papers or pen is being analyzed, assessed, and turned into narrative by not just the lawyers, but the jurors who are equally caught up in their own problems outside of these walls: sick kids, ailing parents, overdue bills, job stress. Regardless of the nature of the case, it's often pretty difficult to keep their attention for the entire time of your testimony, let alone the full trial. If you get too technical, their eyes glaze over with boredom; and if you dumb your responses down too much, you risk annoying them or losing your credibility altogether.

Most of the time, these citizen juries are comprised of people who want to be anywhere but in that courtroom. And so my job, then, is to do something fundamentally paradoxical: to be impartial but persuasive, to be authoritative but unassuming. To be precise, to be authentic, and to earn the jury's trust, case after case, testimony after testimony, without theatrics or lawyerly bravado but with the steadiness of truth.

Why?

Because truth matters. *Justice* matters.

I do this work because somewhere, someone's entire life might hinge on whether I explain something well enough for a jury to truly understand.

And I can't afford to screw up, or second-guess myself, when there's so much at stake.

———

Though not always explicitly labeled as such, expert witnesses have been a cornerstone of Western law since the beginning of the criminal justice system. Records from as far back as the classical period, in ancient Athens, describe physicians summoned to speak about broken bones and the intricate nature of wounds in front of the courts. In the Roman era, courts sought out midwives to explain childbirth, scribes to scrutinize handwriting, and surveyors to resolve boundaries of land. And so it continued, in various iterations across various civilizations, up until 1554, when an English judge described the value of such a specialist in the context of a legal proceeding:

> If matters arise in our law which concern other sciences or faculties, we commonly apply for the aid of that science or faculty which it concerns. Which is an honourable and commendable thing in our law. For thereby it appears that we do not despise all other sciences but our own, but we approve of them and encourage them as things worthy of commendation... In an appeal of mayhem the Judges of our law used to be informed by surgeons whether it be mayhem or not, because their knowledge and skill can best discern it.

It's pretty intuitive, really. If issues arise in a trial that can best be addressed by an expert in any given field, then bring in that expert. *Especially* if the case hinges on confusing or disputed information where the courts lack sufficient context to make informed decisions on their own.

Adhering to basic logic, then, property cases typically brought in surveyors, tax cases brought in bookkeepers, and on and on for different kinds of specialists and tradesmen of direct empirical knowledge, year after year after year. The catch, however, was that this system only worked when experts were neutrally appointed by the court to speak impartially for both sides of the case. Once judges began allowing opposing sides to choose and pay for their own expert witnesses—toward the end of the eighteenth century—the entire premise of impartial experts collapsed. With money came allegiance. And with allegiance came the slow unraveling of objectivity. Who qualified as an expert and to what standards should their expert testimony adhere? No one could say for sure—and that was a big problem.

Simultaneously, there was a massive society-sized shift at the onset of the Industrial Revolution. Science was emerging as a driving factor of economic growth—and consequently, the sudden professionalization of the field meant that courts now faced an equally emergent need for scientific experts to parse the growing complexities of modern disputes.

This was a defining moment, a reimagination of what an expert witness could be. Before, expertise had been tethered to the empirical—a surveyor's lines were clear, an accountant's numbers held true. Now? Expertise was abstract, dealing with theory and the complexities of experiments. A judge could follow a map, but what was he to make of thermodynamics? A jury might comprehend the contours of land, but how could they be expected to make sense of the dense, contradictory tides of scientific testimony? And to make matters worse, even opposing experts tended to disagree, causing courtrooms to become battlegrounds of opposing scientific theories and leading to questions about the validity of science in general. Rising through the turmoil, a popular joke captured public sentiment of the time: "There are three kinds of liars—the common liar, the damned liar, and the scientific expert."

This simmering tension came to a head in the case of *Folkes v. Chadd* (1782), which concerned the deterioration of the harbor in the town of Wells, in northern England, a once-thriving port now rendered useless and inaccessible to ships. Desperate to protect their livelihoods, town residents invested in two artificial sluices that were designed to scour the harbor and keep it operational. However, the sluices failed. And so, looking for somewhere to place the blame, the harbor's board of commissions took legal action against a local landowner, Sir Martin Browne Folkes, alleging that his artificial embankment had disrupted the natural flow of water and, in doing so, choked the harbor.

The question posed to a jury in August 1781 was twofold: Had Folkes's embankment damaged the harbor? And, if so, did that damage warrant its removal? To exactly no one's surprise, the prosecution's opening-day playbook involved a cast of traditional experts—ship captains, mariners, and other men whose expertise was based on empirical observations directly attributable to their training and experience—who were paraded right up to the witness stand, one after the next after the next. One by one, they took the stand, each solemnly affirming that, yes, they had witnessed the harbor's rapid decline firsthand; and that, yes, the harbor's deterioration could be directly attributed to the construction of Folkes's embankment.

To great surprise, however, the landlord's lawyers didn't combat the prosecution with an army of their own traditional experts. Instead, on the second day of the two-day trial, the landlord's lawyers presented a single expert: Robert Mylne, a Fellow of the Royal Society and a famed London-based engineer. Mylne used his time on the stand to explain how the silting of the harbor was due to unseen forces, time's slow erosion, and the confluence of six estuary rivers depositing vast quantities of silt along Norfolk's north coast for years upon years. He then assured the jury that the prosecution's experts weren't lying with their testimony, but that they'd simply mistaken correlation for causation, confusing proximity with proof. The truth, Mylne concluded, did not always reveal itself to the naked eye. It required theory. It required science. And, crucially, it required experts who could see *beyond* the visible and into the hidden mechanisms of nature itself.

To the outrage of Wells's townsfolk, the jury sided with Folkes based on Mylne's persuasive testimony. The harbor's board was in disbelief. In their eyes, Mylne was an outsider who knew nothing about the situation, compared to the intimate knowledge of locals whose entire lives had been shaped by the rhythms of the harbor. Using this as their rationale, the commissioners' lawyers pushed for a new trial "on the ground that the defendants were surprised by the doctrine and reasoning of Mr. Mylne," adding that Mylne's explanations were too theoretical and shouldn't have been permitted in the first place.

Authorities agreed that the commissioners deserved an opportunity to counter Mylne's testimony with expert testimony of their own, stating: "In matters of science, the reasonings of men of science can only be answered by men of science." With that, a new trial was set for the following summer. However, in an attempt to avoid any additional controversy, the judges added a caveat that both parties should pre-exchange, in writing, the opinions of the experts whom they intended to rely on in court "so that both sides might be prepared to answer them." The judges further added, somewhat presciently, an observation that the case "has influenced the whole county of Norfolk, and perhaps the whole country may be affected by it."

As the date for a second trial was set, the harbor commissioners swiftly assembled a team of four well-known experts of scientific rank and regard, whose specialties ranged from engineering to cartography to river navigation and water drainage. Folkes, for his part, hired one additional expert: John Smeaton, a man whose accolade-heavy résumé signaled him as the foremost authority on harbors in all of England. Both sides visited the harbor and conducted research to inform their reports. Both sides then exchanged their findings—first with one another and then with the jury, as directed—and set off to prepare for court. Battle lines had been drawn in the sand.

But something curious happened when the retrial began on July 25, 1782. Though the very premise of the retrial hinged on the commissioners' desire to counter Mylne's scientific testimony with a scientific expert of their own, the exact *opposite* happened. None of the commission's four specifically hired experts were given a chance to testify. Instead, the commission's attorney once again summoned ship captains and mariners to speak about their personal experience of the harbor's deterioration. And when they were finished, the attorney contended that *no* scientific experts, especially Smeaton, should be allowed to address the court, since such testimony would concern the hidden laws of nature and "was matter of opinion, which could be no foundation for the verdict of the jury, which was to be built entirely on facts, and not on opinions."

All of this back-and-forth speaks to the uncertainty surrounding expert testimony at the time. There was no precedent. No guidelines. Just a vacuum where rules should have been, left to be filled by those with the loudest voices or the most persuasive rhetoric. Bias seeped into the cracks, distorting the fragile balance of justice.

This was exactly what happened in the wake of the commission attorney's request to ban scientific experts. The presiding judge, Henry Gould, chief justice of the Royal Court of Common Pleas, accepted the argument that Smeaton's evidence "could be no foundation for the verdict of the jury"—given its hypothetical basis on natural process that would take years to measure, test, or otherwise verify as true. The jury, unsurprisingly, sided with the harbor commission. Equally nonsurprising, Folkes's lawyers refused to let the matter rest. They immediately appealed for a third trial, citing their star witness's improper exclusion. And so it went, back and forth, back and forth—no clear resolution, only the slow grind of bureaucracy, the law stumbling in circles, never quite finding its way.

However, what happened next was a series of events that would become the origin story for the rise of partisan expert testimony in the modern legal system. Where Justice Gould viewed Smeaton's testimony as too speculative for trial, the justice in charge of the third trial, Lord Mansfield, chief justice of the King's Bench, strongly believed that the country's foremost harbor expert should be given the opportunity to speak.

"The question is, to what has this decay been owing?" Mansfield began. "The defendant says, to this bank. Why? Because it prevents the back-water. That is matter of opinion:—the whole case is a question of opinion...I cannot believe that where the question is, whether a defect arises from a natural or an artificial cause, the opinions of men of science are not to be received."

To Lord Mansfield, if the proposed witness was known as an expert on the matter at hand, his opinion should be considered proper evidence. Lord Mansfield's decision marked a transformative moment in the legal landscape. By rejecting the distinction between the expert and his expertise, Mansfield set a standard for the admissibility of scientific matters of opinion. In maintaining that it was not for the court to qualify the expert's opinion, Mansfield's ruling shaped the nineteenth-century practice of expert testimony altogether. If a person was qualified as an expert, his or her expert opinion would be permitted into the courtroom; it was the job of the cross-examiner to expose the weaknesses of the testimony and for the jury to weigh it. Or, as Professor James Thayer of Harvard Law School went on to describe it: Up until Mansfield's decision, "experts were thought of in the old way, as being helpers of the court...But at last the modern conception came in, which regards the expert as testifying, like other witnesses, directly to the jury."

With Smeaton finally allowed to provide his expert testimony, Folkes's team won a decisive victory, one that significantly expanded the scope and standard of experts in courtrooms across the country. And before long, the impact rippled outward, beyond England, beyond the eighteenth century, until it reached American courts, where the role of the expert witness would continue to grow, shaping trials in ways Lord Mansfield himself could scarcely have imagined.*

One of the first notable uses of an expert witness in American history occurred right at the turn of the nineteenth century in New York City. On the night of December 22, 1799, a young woman named Gulielma "Elma" Sands confided in her cousin that she would be leaving the boardinghouse they lived in and eloping with Levi Weeks, a man who had been courting her for several months.

She was never seen or heard from again.

A week and a half later, a young boy informed the authorities that he'd come across some of Sands's possessions, including a muff, near the Manhattan Well (which had recently been constructed in the neighborhood now known as SoHo). After investigating the scene, Sands's body was discovered at the bottom of the well. Rumors immediately started buzzing around town, with speculation that she may have been pregnant at the time of her death.

Suddenly, all eyes were on Levi Weeks.

To combat the media-fueled outrage that was sweeping the city, Levi's older brother Ezra, who'd made a name for himself (and a

---

* It's worth noting that Lord Mansfield was also visionary for his 1772 ruling in *Somerset v. Stewart*, which held that slavery had no basis in English law and that a master could not forcibly remove a slave from England. Widely interpreted as rendering slavery illegal on English soil, the decision became a landmark in the abolitionist movement.

small fortune) in construction, hired several of New York's most prominent attorneys, including Aaron Burr and Alexander Hamilton, to represent his brother at trial. In addition, the defense called upon respected physician and botanist Dr. David Hosack to provide medical expertise regarding the condition of the deceased's body when it was recovered. Hosack openly challenged the prosecution's assertion that Sands had been murdered and thrown into the well shortly after her disappearance, based on his evaluation of the body's bruising and the absence of any signs of a physical confrontation. When both sides finally rested their cases, the jury took only five minutes for deliberation. Weeks was acquitted.

Dr. Hosack's testimony marked a significant moment in American legal history. It added a new dimension to the courtroom, proving that scientific perspective could help juries understand the nuanced specifics of a case as complex and high-profile as Weeks's.

Of course, nothing in law is ever that simple. And while the Weeks case was a huge step toward codifying expert witness as a fundamental aspect of the judicial process, it also sparked fierce debate over who could and couldn't be considered a "competent" expert. Still, in that moment, in that courtroom, with the scent of damp wool coats and the murmurs of the crowd rising like steam, a precedent had been set—and there would be no turning back.

A little over a century later, another case in the U.S. courts would further push the boundaries of expert testimony. It was a time of transition—between wars, between ideas, between a world grasping at modernity and a justice system still anchored to the past.

The case of *Frye v. United States* (1923), in its own way, reflected that shift.

It was more than just a legal proceeding. It was a reckoning.

At the heart of this case was a young man named James Frye, who'd been accused of murdering a prominent doctor. Frye pleaded not guilty, and his legal team, ahead of its time, presented something new to use as evidence in his defense: the results of his systolic blood pressure test (essentially a lie detector test). His lawyer argued that these results were scientific proof of Frye's innocence, and so, William Marston, one of the machine's inventors, was brought in to testify to the validity of these claims.

The court was skeptical from the outset, and the trial judge refused to admit either Marston or his mechanical oracle into evidence, stating: "While courts will go a long way in admitting expert testimony deduced from a well-recognized scientific principle or discovery, the thing from which the deduction is made must be sufficiently established to have gained general acceptance in the particular field in which it belongs."

Without this machine, and without the weight of scientific authority behind him, Frye was swiftly convicted. His lawyer, however, undeterred, appealed the decision, arguing that expert knowledge and scientific evidence had been improperly silenced.

For context, it's important to know that back in 1923, scientific evidence was evaluated according to the traditional evidentiary criteria of the American court system: the "logical relevancy" of the evidence and its helpfulness to the trier of fact, and the qualifications of the witness. In this case, neither criterion offered the Court of Appeals for the District of Columbia much reason to exclude the results of the lie detector test. The logical relevance of the assessment and its potential helpfulness to the jury were obvious. So were the credentials of the test's inventor, William Marston. He was a lawyer, a member of the Massachusetts Bar, and a well-published research psychologist who possessed special training and extensive practical experience pertaining to the subject in question.

After hearing Frye's case, the District of Columbia Court of Appeals allowed for Dr. Marston's testimony, as well as the results of his lie-detector machine, to be presented before the jury. But there was a catch: The court had to evaluate the particular scientific theories and methods on their own merits *before* allowing them to be submitted into evidence.

This was no minor shift. The decision moved beyond the old binary of admit or exclude, trust or reject, and instead framed scientific evidence as something that must first prove itself in its own field before stepping into the courtroom. The jury still remained the final arbiter of facts in a case. Experts were still handpicked by opposing parties. But now the court had extended its role from overseeing the credentials of an individual expert to scrutinizing the credibility of the expertise itself. Thus, the Frye Standard was born, which deems an expert opinion to be admissible if the scientific technique on which the opinion is based is "generally accepted" as reliable in the relevant scientific community. Essentially, it was a safeguard against the allure and seductive promises of new technology that had not yet proven the longevity or legitimacy of its worth.

To many, the initial beauty of the *Frye* ruling lay in its capacity for forward-thinking. It seemed to account for scientific knowledge as an evolutionary process, one that had to advance from experimentation to demonstrable certainty before earning its place in court proceedings. This aligned neatly with the spirit of the times—an era captivated with progress but still wedded to pragmatism. Law, like society, had to adapt, but cautiously, deliberately, in step with the larger changes taking place in the outside world.

———————

Fast-forward to 1975, and all of the initial enthusiasm for *Frye* had soured into criticism and confusion. The so-called general acceptance criterion, once heralded as a valuable safeguard, was now quickly coming to be seen as an unwieldy relic—too vague, too narrow, too burdensome for the courts to constantly adapt, case by case. Many in the legal community had trouble interpreting what "general acceptance" actually meant, or how to apply it with any consistency. And to top it all off, Congress had just further muddied the already murky waters by enacting the Federal Rules of Evidence (FRE). Among its provisions was yet *another* standard for expert testimony: "If scientific, technical, or other specialized knowledge will assist the trier of fact to understand the evidence or to determine a fact in issue, a witness qualified as an expert by knowledge, skill, experience, training, or education, may testify thereto in the form of an opinion or otherwise."

The wording of this standard was broad, flexible, encompassing. But what—critics asked—did it really mean? Was this a reinforcement of the Frye Standard, a quiet replacement, or some strange hybrid of the two? And what about the inevitable exclusions? If courts were now being told to embrace a more open approach to expertise, how could they ensure problematic and/or inconsistent methods were kept out?

In trying to fix the problem, FRE had only added new layers of ambiguity. The law was modernizing, yes, but in a way that replaced one set of questions with another—questions that would demand years of litigation, reinterpretation, and revision before any real answers emerged. The whole situation was untenable. Something needed to give.

This conflict came to a head with the 1993 trial of *Daubert v. Merrell Dow Pharmaceuticals*, in which plaintiffs Jason Daubert and Eric Schuller, both born with serious birth defects, took on pharmaceutical giant Merrell Dow, claiming that their mothers' prenatal use of the drug company's popular anti-nausea medicine, Bendectin, had been the direct cause of their conditions. The case had all the markings of a modern fable: a David-versus-Goliath matchup that pitted the vulnerable against the powerful, the individual against the institution, a demand for truth against a wall of corporate greed.

During the initial civil trial, the plaintiffs' attorneys leaned heavily on a strategy that favored expert testimony. They enlisted eight well-credentialed specialists (a team of scientists and doctors) to prove a causal link between the drug and the birth defects based on three key findings: animal studies that found links between Bendectin and malformation; chemical analysis that pointed to structural similarities between Bendectin and other substances known to cause birth defects; and reanalysis of previously published epidemiological data that found a link between the drug and birth defects.

Surprisingly, despite the wealth of evidence provided, the

federal judge was unmoved. Animal studies, he stated, were too indirect. Chemical analysis? Too abstract. The meta-analysis of epidemiological data? Not peer-reviewed, not published, not "generally accepted." *Frye's* "general acceptance" principle reigned, and by that measure, the evidence that provided the foundation of the prosecution's case did not belong in court. The judge granted summary judgment to Merrell Dow, dismissing the case before it even reached a jury.

Determined to have their evidence included, Daubert's lawyers took their appeal all the way to the Supreme Court. They argued that FRE had long since overtaken *Frye* and therefore superseded *Frye*, and that it was the purview of a jury, not a judge, to determine the persuasiveness of scientific evidence. The Supreme Court agreed—in part. *Frye* had been misapplied, yes, but the Court rejected the idea that all scientific evidence should simply be allowed in and left to the jury's discretion. There had to be a threshold, a mechanism to filter the valid from the dubious. And it was a judge's job, the Court ruled, to filter out inadequate evidence that the jury didn't need to see. That said, the Court acknowledged the need for a clear framework to guide judges in determining the relevance and reliability of future expert testimony.

And so, with no clear-cut formula to determine scientific validity, the Court devised a flexible assessment of its own. It was a courageous dip into the murky waters of modern philosophy and science that they prefaced with a caveat: "We are confident that federal judges possess the capacity to undertake this review. Many factors will bear on the inquiry, and we do not presume to set out a definitive checklist or test." The Court then offered guidelines in the form of five nonexclusive questions that could be universally applied:

- Can the expert's technique or theory be tested and assessed for reliability?
- Has the technique or theory been subjected to peer review and publication?
- What is its known or potential error rate?
- Are there standards for this technique?
- Has the technique or theory been generally accepted in the scientific community?

Ultimately, *Daubert* changed everything, compelling the courts to abandon *Frye*'s rigid "general acceptance" principle in favor of a more nuanced, judge-driven inquiry. More important, *Daubert* gave the legal system a long-overdue federal standard for evaluating expert testimony.

There was, however, one lingering question that still remained unresolved: Did *Daubert* apply only to "scientific and technical" testimony, as FRE indicated, or did its reach extend even further? The answer came in *Kumho Tire Co. v. Carmichael*, when the U.S. Supreme Court held that *Daubert* applied to all expert witness testimony—scientific, technical, or otherwise. This gave judges the power to consider factors beyond *Daubert*'s five questions if they helped filter out unreliable testimony. It also gave them an unprecedented level of scrutiny, turning them into gatekeepers who protected the sanctity of the courtroom by excluding phony and fraudulent "expertise."

And this, for me, is where it became personal.

From the very beginning of my career, I have advocated for victims of sexual abuse, trauma, and violence. It's painstaking work, delicate and brutal all at once. And it taught me early on that the only way to help victims—whether taking their initial statements to law enforcement or validating the extent of their trauma in front of a jury—is through methods that are firmly grounded in fact. It's not enough to have noble intentions. You need proof: a solid scientific foundation so unshakable that no clever defense attorney, no overworked judge, can sweep it aside with a dash of their pen.

And so this is what I fight for. When the stakes are this high, when people's lives hang in the balance, there can be no room for error. The line between justice and failure is drawn in the sharp clarity of evidence. Everything else is just noise.

CHAPTER 1

Justice for Jane

My first encounter with the American legal system took place in the early '70s. A lot was different back then. Court cases hadn't yet transformed into the media spectacles we see today. They rarely drew TV crews or national reporters or the wide-eyed curiosity of an insatiable public demanding to know each gritty detail of human behavior in its most abject form.

In fact, throughout much of the twentieth century, trials stayed secreted away behind courtroom walls, leaving the courts free to operate within their own devices. This had its benefits, to be sure. For the jury, lawyers, and expert witnesses like myself, the lack of scrutiny allowed us to focus solely on the facts of a case, ensuring that we wouldn't be distracted by the sideshow of a media presence. But the absence of outside influence had its drawbacks, too. It made the legal system stagnant, insular—an exact inverse to the social and cultural revolution taking place so rapidly in 1970s America.

In other words, times were changing—and the court system was failing to keep up.

Of course, I didn't have this clarity of perspective back then. I was still finding my path as a recent graduate of a PhD nursing program, now in the early stages of my career. That path led me to a research project that was focused on understanding the emotional and traumatic effects of rape and sexual assault. And although trials were a small offshoot of the project, they quickly grew into something more all-encompassing.

You see, in the 1970s, sexual violence had become one of the four major crimes in the United States. And yet, somehow—infuriatingly—it had the lowest conviction rate of *any* crime. It was a silent epidemic—rarely talked about, investigated even less, and almost never seen in court. It was shocking. I could hardly believe that such a systemic failure was hiding in plain sight. But once I wrapped my head around the scope of the problem—mostly by interviewing victims and learning about the nuanced nature of their trauma—I realized that if I wanted to see any kind of change represented in society at large, I needed to follow this process through. And, for me, that meant providing crisis counseling to victims, developing trauma-informed protocols for law enforcement, and standing alongside those rare survivors whose cases somehow beat the odds and made it through to trial.

That's what brought me to Jane. Her case was one of the 2 to 5 percent of sexual assault cases that made it to trial at the start of the decade. She'd been raped by three men who'd forced their way into her apartment in the fall of 1973. Crucially, within the first forty-eight hours after the attack, a responding detective named Paul Rufo made two prescient decisions. The first was having Jane write down every single detail she could remember about what happened and the three men who attacked her.

"It will be helpful for your case," he said.

The second was telling Jane there was someone she should speak to. That's how I got involved. I was introduced to Jane by phone, and the two of us talked for nearly an hour. We then made plans to continue crisis counseling at a regular cadence for as long as she needed.

Jane was severely traumatized. She'd protectively walled herself off, and it took her some time to really open up to me, which was certainly understandable. Slowly, over the course of several months, she told me all about the attack, about her family's lack of support—"You must have done something wrong," they said, "rape doesn't just *happen*"—and about feeling like an imposter in her own skin. She described wanting to disappear. To give up.

"This attack doesn't define you," I reminded her. "I know it feels like it does. But that's just temporary. Healing takes time."

As the leaves fell and the season changed, I made sure to check in on Jane more often. Holidays, with their relentless stimulation, can be triggering for people with trauma. So we set up a schedule—a routine to hold on to—and, for the most part, we stuck to it. But on the day after Christmas, she surprised me with a call out of the blue.

"You'll never believe this," she told me. "I just got off the phone with Detective Rufo. There's been an arrest. Actually, *three* arrests. And they recovered some of my stuff from one of the men's homes. Apparently, the investigating officer knew one of the men's families. He made the arrest and then had to tell the parents about the charges. And it wasn't just me, either. There were other victims. He raped a six-year-old child, a forty-five-year-old woman, and an eighty-year-old woman."

I didn't know what to say. The numbers were stacked so high against her, against anyone—with less than 80 percent of rape cases reported, and less than 30 percent of those reported cases ending in arrest. I understood the fragile hope she was clinging to, the thin thread of possibility that something good might emerge from this horror. So I listened as she spoke about the call and the opportunity to pursue charges. She had a rare chance at finding justice. But justice, I knew, wasn't a clean thing. It would come at the cost of reliving her trauma for an entire courtroom to hear. It would be a difficult choice.

"What are you going to do?" I asked, keeping my voice as neutral as possible.

"I'm going to finish this," she said. "I'm going to take them to court."

I should pause for a moment here.

Context is important, and it's necessary to point out that if Jane's case had happened today, there's a good likelihood that she'd be supported by the media and a sympathetic public—given the current entertainment appeal of court cases and cultural fascination with true crime. But none of that existed back in the 1970s. There were no podcasts with massive followings. No digital infrastructure to gather like-minded individuals whom traditional media left behind. Cases like Jane's went unseen, unheard, unknown. And yes, it was extraordinary that she'd defied the odds to make it through to trial. But was that newsworthy? Apparently not. Because despite how many coins I fed into the brightly colored newspaper boxes lining the city streets on my way to work, I found little more than a passing mention of Jane's story—if anything at all.

This wasn't a surprise. Particularly since the world at the time was preoccupied with presidential impeachment proceedings, civil rights coverage, and the horrors of the Vietnam War. With very little precedent for trial coverage to begin with, there was simply no way a case like Jane's could compete with all the other uncertainty vying for headlines.

Even so, change was coming. It was simmering in the staticky glow of recently colorized TVs. It was rising with the shift to an era of twenty-four-hour news cycles. By this point, it had been building and building for a hundred years—its origins traceable back to a single legal decision: *Patterson v. Colorado* (1907).

Patterson was a milestone case in the history of American jurisprudence, one that centered around freedom of speech and freedom of press and whether these rights existed on either a state or federal level. The specifics had to do with a criminal contempt citation brought against a newspaper owner and former senator, Thomas M. Patterson, who'd been charged with printing articles and cartoons that mocked the seemingly politically motivated decisions made by the Colorado Supreme Court. After being convicted, Patterson appealed the decision but lost the case again when the United States Supreme Court upheld Colorado's ruling. Rationalizing its decision, the Court explained that what constituted "contempt" was a matter of local law, and that individual states were perfectly within their rights to rule on contempt without infringing upon the Constitution. And although free speech and free press were protected from abridgment by the Constitution, the Court added, this did not exempt them from subsequent punishment if their contents were deemed contrary to public interest. Delivering the Court's ruling, associate justice Oliver Wendell Holmes clearly stated: "The theory of our system is that the conclusions to be reached in a case will be induced only by evidence and argument in open court, and not by any outside influence, whether of private talk or public print."

The implications of this decision were profound. In effect, it placed a muzzle on the majority of American newspapers for the next twenty-plus years. This dystopian reality weighed heavy on the media landscape until *Near v. Minnesota* (1931) forced the Supreme Court to step back and reconsider its position. Much like *Patterson*, *Near* called into question whether freedom of the press existed at a state level or as a constitutional guarantee. However, when this case was brought to trial, the U.S. Supreme Court one-eightied from its *Patterson* decision and ruled that press freedom was protected within the First Amendment and applied to the states through the Fourteenth Amendment. In delivering this decision, Supreme Court Chief Justice Charles Evans Hughes affirmed: "It is no longer open to doubt that the liberty of the press and of speech is within the liberty safeguarded by the due process clause of the Fourteenth Amendment from invasion by state action." In other words, the muzzle was off. Neither states nor the federal government had any rights to compromise freedom of the press or freedom of speech.

It's hard to overstate how important this ruling was. Just ask any legal scholar and they'll tell you that *Near v. Minnesota* is as fundamentally American as warm apple pie. But its impact wasn't a flip of the switch. Twenty-plus years of *Patterson* had forced newspapers to adapt. Caution and discretion had become deeply ingrained in American journalism. And in those decades of limited freedoms, something like a truce had developed between the courts and the media to prevent prejudicial spillover from seeping into the streets.

It was simple, really. Even in the wake of *Near*, the conditioning effect of *Patterson* meant that trial coverage took a back seat to things like politics, social upheavals, stock market speculation, foreign affairs, and the rise of consumer culture and mass entertainment. The few trials that garnered coverage were done so sparingly—unadorned by sensationalism or the depths of graphic detail we've come to expect today.

This pattern continued throughout the 1930s, '40s, and '50s with rare exception. It was self-reinforcing in nature—the lack of trial coverage led to public apathy toward trials, which in turn led to lack of trial coverage, which then led to further public apathy, and on and on the cycle kept chugging forward.

But then, in 1966, with the release of Truman Capote's *In Cold Blood*, something awakened in the American psyche that had long been dormant. Murder grabbed hold of the public's collective imagination once again. The true crime epic told the story of the Clutter family, who were murdered in their rural Kansas home by two recently paroled former convicts in a botched burglary attempt. Through the use of firsthand interviews and investigative documents, Capote had effectively created a new way of bringing readers inside the minds and emotions of killers and their victims. It was fascinating. It was terrifying. And it was all grounded in a real case and the ensuing psychological unraveling that played out in court. With *In Cold Blood*, Capote set the stage for an entirely new genre of true crime and celebrity trials that would grow exponentially in the decades to come.

Timing wise, Capote's release of *In Cold Blood* was somewhat of a portent. It set the stage for what historian Harold Schechter designated "the Golden Age of Serial Murder," which started in the late 1960s with offenders like the Zodiac Killer and Charles Manson, and which continued to dominate headlines throughout the '70s and '80s with the likes of Ted Bundy, John Wayne Gacy, Son of Sam, the Hillside Strangler, and on and on. The chronology was captivating. A once-fringe phenomenon had swelled into a pop culture obsession—seemingly overnight. Murder took center stage once more and dominated the nation's papers. Trial analysis became a fixture on the nightly news. Radio scanners sold out at record highs as a fearful public sought to keep tabs on the latest investigations. The whole thing was everywhere all at once. But there was a catch. Only serial killers seemed to get any real media recognition. Most other trials were largely ignored. And as for victims of sexual violence? No chance. Their cases hardly even seemed to exist.

It wasn't until the late fall of 1974 that the first media reports of a high-profile rape case grabbed those top headlines. The victim was actress and singer Connie Francis. She was beautiful and talented and had climbed her way to an international level of fame. In November of that year, during a multinight appearance at the Westbury Music Fair in Jericho, New York, Francis was awakened by a stranger who broke into her room at the Howard Johnson Motor Lodge and then proceeded to rape her at knifepoint for nearly three hours. The man then tied Francis's hands behind her back and covered her with two mattresses.

Immediately after Francis freed herself and reported the attack, police were brought in to analyze the scene. Reporters soon followed. And despite the sordid nature of the case, the papers, chasing after Francis's celebrity appeal, quickly published one article after the next with the now all-too-familiar trope of an innocent young woman's picture juxtaposed against a headline of rape and violence. Her case became one of the most publicized crimes of the year. It also led to Francis having a nervous breakdown, which ended her marriage and caused her to become a recluse for nearly a decade. Quietly, however, she did sue the hotel chain and was awarded a reported $2.5 million. At the time, this was one of the largest such judgments in history, leading to widespread reform in hotel security.

I've always felt that one of the most important takeaways from the Francis case was the fact that it evoked such deep public empathy. This was a stark contrast to how rape cases had been treated in the past. Rather than the typical response of victim blaming or pretending the issue didn't exist, Connie Francis was supported. She was rallied around. And while these simple acts of compassion may seem small and inconsequential by today's standards, they stood out as something wholly unprecedented at the time.

That tiny shift in public mentality—coupled with the aura of celebrity Francis brought to the case—suddenly broke open the floodgates. The nascent phenomenon of true crime was now capturing the imagination of a far broader audience than just the serial-killer aficionados of the past. There was now interest in victims. Finally, the public was ready to hear their side of the story.

Not just the sensationalism of the crime itself, but the larger truth of who these victims were and how their stories might end.

This was the turning point. The Francis case humanized the genre of true crime, transforming it from mere spectacle into something intimate, something that pricked at the nation's collective conscience. Justice, the public was beginning to see, was a moral imperative. Accountability mattered. Victims mattered. And in order to ensure that justice was carried out, the American legal system needed to step up.

———

Set back the clock eleven months, however, and Jane was on her own with the courts. It was January 1974, and she had just come face-to-face with her offenders at the probable cause hearing for the first time since the attack.

"It was almost surreal," she recalled afterward, during our call. "I couldn't believe how small the gunman was. He'd been this looming presence in my mind for months. And then there he was, this tiny and insignificant in person."

She had sounded so optimistic when she first told me she was going to take the attacker to court. But her outlook soured in the weeks leading up to her first day in court.

"It feels like I'm the one being put on trial," she admitted. "They made me sit right next to the men's families. It was awful. They kept asking why I was doing this, and couldn't I see that I was ruining their sons' lives."

I had to take a minute to really process that.

Because as unimaginable as it may sound today—the idea of

a victim, sitting alone in court, getting hissed at by the offender's family—*that* was the grim reality faced by far too many women over the decades. We lived within a cultural landscape tailored to and by men, our value secondary to theirs. There was no balance of power, no threat of accountability in the eyes of the law. There was simply a prevailing social attitude empowering men to treat women however they might want.

"I know," I said, struggling to find something more meaningful to say. But the whole situation was overwhelming. Jane would have to relive her trauma all over again for an entire courtroom to see—and I was powerless to help her. Despite my experience working with countless survivors of sexual trauma, and despite all the professional work I'd done specifically with Jane, neither the judge nor the lawyers had asked me to submit a psychiatric report or provide any sort of expert role in the proceedings whatsoever.

What was worse, I don't think they did this intentionally. I think it was due to a far simpler and far more frustrating reality— I was a woman in the male-dominated culture of the 1970s. I'm sure no one even considered the *possibility* that I could help.

"Listen," I said. "Try and get some rest. Tomorrow will be a better day."

It was past midnight when we got off the phone. I had classes to teach the following morning, but I knew I wouldn't get much sleep. What was the point? I'd been naïve to think I could shift cultural perceptions with research alone. My work was important— I believed that—but so what? Plenty of important work fails to make a wider public impact. Only the rare few manage to break through the inaccessible threshold of academia. I didn't yet have the answers, but I knew I needed to do *something*.

And so, the following morning, when Jane arrived at the courthouse to be sworn in at 10:40 a.m., I was standing right there behind her, in the front row, accompanied by every single student from my 9:00 a.m. class.

Whether or not it would have any real impact on the case itself—this was the right thing to do. I wanted Jane to know, to *see*, that she wasn't alone in this fight. That someone believed in her. That someone was willing to stand beside her, even when the system made her feel small.

And as I stood there, I realized something deeper as well. If I truly wanted to support victims moving forward—not just in this case but in all the cases that would come next—I needed my voice to carry weight. I needed to establish myself as an official expert witness.

Because here's the thing: Justice is an imagined construct, and so it matters who imagines it. Who defines it. Who enforces it. And who's willing to challenge it when it fails.

I knew I couldn't change the system overnight, and I couldn't guarantee that every victim would receive the justice they deserved. But I could do something. I could contextualize their experiences and share everything I knew about trauma with the people who had the power to make a lasting judicial impact: the juries.

And maybe, just maybe, that would be enough to tip the scales.

CHAPTER 2

Meeting Erik Menendez

Emergency Dispatcher: "Beverly Hills emergency."

Caller: "Yes, ah, um."

Dispatcher: "What's the problem?"

Caller: "Ah."

Dispatcher: "What's the problem? What's the problem?"

Caller: "Someone killed my parents."

Dispatcher: "Pardon me?"

Caller: "Someone killed my parents."

Dispatcher: "What—who? Are they still there?"

Caller: "Yes."

Dispatcher: "The people who killed them?"

Caller: "What? No, no, no."

Dispatcher: "Were they shot?"

Caller: "Yes."

Dispatcher: "They were shot."

Caller: "Yes."

(Muffled sound of dispatcher giving orders on another line.
   Shouting in the background from the caller's end.)
Caller: "Shut up! Erik, shut up. Erik, shut up!"
. . .
Dispatcher: "Who is the person that was shot?"
Caller: "My mom and my dad."
Dispatcher: "Your mom and dad?"
Caller: "My mom and dad."
Dispatcher: "Okay. Hold on a second."
Caller: (sobbing)
Dispatcher: "We're on our way over there with an ambulance."
Caller: (sobbing)

On a normal night, Elm Drive was quietly opulent. Its coveted multimillion-dollar mansions felt sheltered and exclusive beyond even the surrounding splendor of Beverly Hills. But on the evening of August 20, 1989, a rush of flashing lights and sirens ripped through the calm as police converged outside of a five-million-dollar residence. Neighbors peered over privacy hedges, their curiosity insatiable.

Cutting through the chaos were the muffled sobs of eighteen-year-old Erik Menendez, who was rocking back and forth in a fetal position on the mansion's front lawn. Nearby, Erik's twenty-one-year-old brother, Lyle Menendez, was screaming and running around, uncontrollable with grief.

Inside the house, investigators were shocked to discover the lifeless bodies of José and Mary Louise "Kitty" Menendez, blood pooling beneath them thanks to a barrage of blasts from a twelve-gauge shotgun. José was shot five times; fragments of his skull were splattered across the room. His wife, however, had been hit nine times—including one that blasted away her nose and eye, rendering her nearly unrecognizable.

The crime scene was so brutal that initial descriptions characterized it as a "gangland-style" killing, but the rest of the facts just didn't add up: Investigators found no signs of forced entry, no shell casings to collect forensics from, and nothing that pointed to a robbery. Interestingly, however, the crime *did* feature a ritualistic element, something that might be considered a possible signature—as both victims had been shot directly in the kneecaps.

"Do you know anyone who would want to do this to your parents?" an investigator asked the brothers.

"Maybe the mob," Lyle suggested, his voice breaking with despair.

Investigators didn't ask many more questions than that. In fact, the brothers' grief was so convincing, so *consuming*, that investigators didn't follow the standard protocol of testing Erik's and Lyle's hands and clothing for gunshot residue.

And why would they? After all, the Menendez brothers weren't considered suspects—at least, not initially. They were grieving kids. So instead, law enforcement turned their focus toward José's business rivals, theorizing that one of them must be to blame for these senseless killings.

———

Despite extensive media coverage and a stirring of widespread public fascination, I knew very little about the murders of José and Kitty Menendez—until I received a call from a man named Jon Conte in April 1990.

Jon, an academic and a social worker, was a pioneer in the field of sexual violence. The two of us got to know each other over the years in a way that's typical for academics: We followed the same conference circuit and shared a number of professional acquaintances, including Jim Cooney, who'd pulled me into the Henry Louis Wallace case in the first place. Jon admired my work with the FBI, and I admired his work as founding editor of the *Journal of Interpersonal Violence*. We talked often, so I wasn't surprised to see his name appear on my phone. But I had no idea where this particular call would lead me.

"What do you mean you haven't been following the Menendez murders?" he asked. "This case is like a Hollywood script playing out in real time. The media's been going on and on about it nonstop. How have you *not* been following it?"

"Work keeps me busy," I said with a shrug. "Why do you ask?"

"Because I've been brought on to testify for the defense. And I think your insight could be valuable here, too. There's a whole element of delayed disclosure and child abuse. I'm the expert for Lyle, but we need someone to interview and assess Erik. I already told their defense attorney, Leslie Abramson, about you."

"How old are these kids?"

There was a pause on Jon's end before he responded.

"Look—go out and buy the March 26 issue of *People* magazine. It's the one with the purple cover. Read the story about the two brothers who've been accused of shooting their parents. If you're interested, let me know. Leslie will want to fly you out to

LA to meet you in person. She's something, Leslie is. I think you two will really hit it off."

Jon was right. The Menendez case read like a script of the American dream gone horribly wrong. It started with José—born and raised in Cuba—being sent to the United States at the age of sixteen, hoping for a better life in the aftermath of the Cuban Revolution. José lived in the attic of a cousin's home for a while, then attended college at Southern Illinois University at Carbondale on a swimming scholarship. Ultimately, he stuck with the team for only a year before quitting, marrying Kitty Andersen (a beauty pageant queen who'd caught his eye in debate class) and moving to New York to earn a degree in accounting from Queens College.

After arriving in New York, José's career took off at a dizzying pace. He landed a job with the Manhattan firm Coopers & Lybrand, leapfrogged to head of commercial leasing for Hertz, and continued up the ladder to the record division of RCA, where he signed iconic musicians, including Menudo, the Eurythmics, and Duran Duran. Then, in 1986, when he was passed over for the executive vice presidency of RCA Records, José uprooted his young family—Kitty and their two sons, Erik and Lyle—and moved to LA after being offered a corporate executive position at International Video Entertainment. José's dedication and business savvy earned the company $8 million by the end of his first year, and nearly $16 million the year after that.

As demanding as he was driven, José applied the same degree of intensity toward raising his sons. He enrolled them in elite private schools, hired tutors, and enforced a strict regime of private tennis lessons—often starting at 6:00 a.m.—regardless of holidays, illness, or bad weather.

"We are prototypes of my father," Erik later explained. "He wanted us to be exactly like him."

To outsiders, the Menendez family cut the perfect picture. They were young, wealthy, and devoted to each other, with friends describing them as an "extraordinarily close-knit" unit. Neighbors admired Kitty for attending every tennis and soccer match her boys played, José for rushing home each night to have dinner with his family, and the family as a whole for their lavish vacations and luxe lifestyle. But appearances are often deceiving, and lurking beneath that flawless façade were numerous signs that something wasn't quite right with the household.

For starters, the brothers both had a rebellious streak. Erik lashed out by burglarizing the homes of his parents' friends, while Lyle struggled academically at Princeton and was suspended for plagiarism. While José was *irate* with both sons, he still used his money and influence to help shield them as best he could. Consequently, Erik's felony charges—including grand theft burglary—were dropped, and he got off relatively lightly with a sentence of community service time and a court requirement to undergo psychological counseling with therapist Dr. Jerome Oziel. Meanwhile, Lyle was allowed to return to school following the cheating scandal, and he began seeing Dr. Oziel as well. Despite their desire to protect their sons, both parents were well aware of their children's flaws. Kitty, who was undergoing counseling for her own issues at the time, confided in her therapist that she believed the boys were "narcissistic, lacked conscience, and exhibited signs that they were sociopaths."

On August 20, 1989, just two weeks after Kitty made this statement to her therapist, José and Kitty Menendez were found murdered in the television room of their LA home. The crime scene was like something out of a horror movie. As one investigator recalled: "I've seen a lot of homicides, but nothing quite that brutal. Blood, flesh, skulls. It would be hard to describe, especially José, as resembling a human that you would recognize. *That's* how bad it was."

In the weeks following this barbaric double homicide, investigators noticed that Erik and Lyle weren't exactly acting like typical kids mourning the loss of their parents. For starters, they were spending a *lot* of money—and fast. Lyle purchased a Rolex, a Porsche, and a successful restaurant, while Erik bought a Jeep Wrangler, hired a $50,000 personal tennis coach, and got scammed out of $40,000 by a con artist who tricked him into investing in a rock concert that never happened. They also rented adjoining penthouse condos in LA's sought-after Marina del Rey community, which they used as home base between excursions to London, the Caribbean, and Lake Tahoe.

Still, it wasn't until several months of dead ends and red herrings that investigators began to grow increasingly suspicious about the brothers' presumed innocence. This coincided with an incident where a family member found a reference to a recently revised will on José's home computer, but before a specialist could be brought in to retrieve the document, Lyle happened to erase it "by mistake." The computer specialist, however, said he didn't believe it was an accident, claiming "in my opinion, there was another program used to clean the hard disk."

The more police dug into the brothers' postcrime behavior,

the more odd "coincidences" they uncovered—like a movie script cowritten by Erik that featured eerie parallels to the August 20 murders. *Friends*, as the script was titled, chronicled the story of eighteen-year-old Hamilton Cromwell, a man who murders his wealthy parents in order to inherit $157 million. One quote in particular, in which Cromwell explains his disdain for his father, seemed to echo statements that the brothers made about José: "Sometimes, he would tell me that I was not worthy to be his son. When he did that, it would make me strive harder... just so I could hear the words, 'I love you, son.'... And I never heard those words."

Despite all the red flags and circumstantial evidence, investigators still needed something solid to build their case around—until finally, on March 5, 1990, they got the tip they needed. That afternoon, Judalon Smyth—an ex-mistress of Erik and Lyle's psychologist, Jerome Oziel—contacted Beverly Hills police to alert them to the existence of confessions that Dr. Oziel had recorded during sessions in his office. Smyth, who had listened to these confessions for herself, learned a great deal from the audio, which was recorded between October 31 and November 2, 1989. She knew, for example, that the murder weapons had been purchased at a sporting-goods store in San Diego. And she also knew that the brothers had threatened to kill Oziel if he went to the authorities.

Three days after Smyth's tip-off, Lyle was arrested while leaving the family home on Elm Drive. More than a dozen police officers swarmed in, forced him to lie down in the street, handcuffed him, escorted him to the police station, and then booked him on suspicion of murder. Erik was arrested three days later. He'd been playing in a tennis tournament overseas at the time. But after hearing about his brother, he immediately packed his things and flew back from Israel to Miami, where an aunt advised him to turn himself in. He took her advice and returned to LA, where he was met at the airport by four detectives, driven straight to the Los Angeles County Men's Central Jail, and then held without bond.

————

I set the article aside to consider what I'd read.

It wasn't subtle. That much was clear. The writer hadn't held back in assigning accusation, motive, or blame. Nor had they been shy about picking the low-hanging narrative of murder for money by "two handsome sons...the sole beneficiaries of their parents' estimated $14 million estate."

But that didn't add up. Erik and Lyle were already rich. Why jeopardize their Hollywood lifestyle by killing their parents for money when money was something they already had? And the sheer brutality of the crime didn't make sense, either. Repeatedly shooting their parents in the heads? It wasn't just extreme; it was *personal*.

And on top of that, I couldn't quite figure out why the defense was interested in my specific expertise. Why bother with an academic expert who specialized in cases of sexual violence and abuse, rather than someone more experienced in this type of high-profile, media-fueled celebrity murder trial?

Even so, my curiosity was piqued—and I was interested to learn more about the brothers and their complicated family dynamic.

"Okay Jon," I said, calling him back the next afternoon. "I'm in. I can be on a plane as early as next week."

———————

On the flight to LA, I decided to prepare for the meeting by reading everything I could on the brothers' representative, Leslie Abramson. Of course, I already knew bits and pieces of her biography. She was a trailblazer who'd made the leap from public defender to opening her own private practice and twice being named the LA Criminal Courts Bar Association's trial lawyer of the year. Her meteoric rise to fame included the defense of seventeen-year-old Arnel Salvatierra, who killed his father in his sleep after suffering years of physical abuse, as well as the defense of Dr. Khalid Parwez, a gynecologist arrested in 1987 on allegations of strangling and dismembering his eleven-year-old son during a bitter custody dispute. The incendiary nature of these cases, along with the take-no-prisoners tactics she employed on her clients' behalf, made her a polarizing figure. *Vanity Fair* lauded Abramson as "the most brilliant Los Angeles defense lawyer for death-row cases"; the *Los Angeles Times*, on the other hand, described her as a "4-foot-11, fire-eating, mudslinging, nuclear-strength pain in the legal butt."

As someone who shared the distinction of being called a pain in the butt simply for having an uncompromising work ethic, I was willing to hear Leslie out. And I was further intrigued that she'd invited me to stay at her home rather than putting me up in a hotel—most lawyers prefer to maintain as much professional aloofness as possible. Of course, I had no idea what I was getting myself into. But all the zigzags and redirections throughout my career had taught me one thing: It's best to keep an open mind.

Leslie was waiting for me at the airport when my flight touched down in LA. In a radical departure from her media portrayal as a fire-eating terror, she greeted me warmly, with kindness and good humor. In fact, as we piled into her car and plowed our way through traffic en route to her residence, I might've forgotten the fact that we'd been brought together by the biggest criminal case in years—if not for the constant ringing of her car phone. It was *incessant*.

I remember thinking to myself, *This is going to be a wild ride.*

Once we arrived at her house, Leslie gave me a minute to get settled before diving right into the case. She explained that she'd been hesitant about reaching out to me at first, until she talked with Paul Mones, a children's rights advocate who quite literally wrote the book about abused children who murder their parents. It was only then that she began to realize the deeply nuanced psychological elements underpinning the Menendez murders.

"I found the conversation with Mones pretty compelling," she told me. "He recognized similarities between this case and other childhood abuse cases right away. A lot of what he said made sense—like how abused children tend to suffer in silence until they snap and fight back, often to the point of overkill, shooting an abuser again and again. But I needed to be certain. So, I hired Dr. William Vicary—he's a local psychiatrist, I'm not sure if you've heard of him—to meet with Erik in person. That's when Erik opened up about the abuse he'd experienced for years. His story changed everything."

I nodded, taking it all in. I wasn't exactly surprised by this detail, but I still needed a moment or two to process everything I'd heard.

"As shocking as it was," Leslie continued, "everything in this case has been exactly as Mones explained it to me. The psychological twisting by the parents. The years of abuse behind closed doors. All that pushing and pressure—until finally, the boys reached a breaking point. Lyle cracked first when he flunked out of Princeton. Then the parents used Lyle's failure against Erik and refused to let him attend college out of state. But that was the final straw. It was all just too much. And the boys exploded."

"That's fairly typical with these types of cases," I replied. "I've seen it over and over throughout my career. The pressure eventually finds a release. Not necessarily the same level of violence, but the same behavioral patterns."

"Right," Leslie agreed. "At which point, the case is no longer about individual responsibility. It's about people getting caught up in events and acting precisely how you'd expect them to."

"That's one way of looking at it," I said. "But it's hard to understand someone's individual responsibility without first assessing their overall mental well-being. That's the overlap between psychology and profiling. You have to look for patterns in a case like this. Take the fifteen gunshots found at the scene, for example. That's excessive. And the way all the shots targeted specific parts of the body—that speaks to a whole different scope of emotion than just anger or rage. It speaks to fear."

"Fear, threat, pressure—they blew up." Leslie sighed. "Here's the thing, Ann. I'm fully convinced that Erik and Lyle aren't totally responsible for becoming the people that they turned out to be, for doing the horrible things they ended up doing. It was these horrible circumstances that molded them into the men they are today. From all the reading I've done, from talking to Erik and Lyle themselves, I'm pretty convinced of that. But I also want your expert opinion. If we see things differently, that's okay. But I do want to make sure I'm building the best team I can for my clients here, and I want everyone to be on the same page."

"Will I be able to speak with Erik beforehand?" I asked. "That's going to be necessary if you want an honest assessment."

"Of course," she said. "For the sake of transparency, though, I do need to disclose this: You're not the first expert I've consulted. I flew in a Harvard professor last week, before Jon mentioned you and your credentials. But it just wasn't a good fit. She met with Erik, spoke with him briefly, then suggested a defense structured around a folie à deux—what she described as a shared psychosis or delusional disorder where hallucinations can pass from one person to another. I appreciated her time, but I find that theory pretty unrealistic. So I sent her back to Boston."

"What makes you think you won't be sending me back, too?"

"Jon, for one thing. Your experience, for another. It's not just the fact that you've spent so much time working with the FBI to develop criminal profiling and interview violent offenders; it's that *combined* with your perspective as a forensic psychiatric nurse. That checks a lot of boxes for me. I didn't even know forensic nurses existed, but you've studied victims of abuse, you've studied the mentally disturbed, *and* you've studied what makes serial killers tick. You know how to get into people's minds. I need someone who knows how to do that. I need someone who can tell me exactly why Erik and Lyle killed their parents that day. I need *you*."

———————

The next day, I met Erik in a small visitation room at the Los Angeles County men's jail. He was led in wearing a jumpsuit, leg cuffs, and wrist chains that were quickly locked down to the table in front of me.

"Hello, Erik," I said. "I'm Ann Burgess. I'm a professor and a nurse with specialties in trauma, abuse, and behavioral psychology, and I'm here on behalf of your attorney. I'm looking forward to talking with you this morning."

He stared me up and down for a moment before wincing and turning away.

As eager as I was to speak with him, I held back, giving him the space to steer the conversation if he chose. I wanted him to feel at ease, to settle into the moment without pressure. A minute passed, then another, the silence stretching between us until he finally cleared his throat and asked about my flight. We talked a bit about Los Angeles and the traffic on the freeways. He was clearly interested in focusing the conversation on nonthreatening parts of his life, so I followed his lead and asked a general question about how he was doing, all things considered.

He shrugged. "Prison isn't so bad. At least, not compared to how they show it on TV. The food's okay, there's an exercise room, and I've been getting visits and calls from a lot of family members. Lyle's here, too, and they let us see each other pretty frequently."

I wanted our conversation to focus on him—and not his brother—so I followed up by asking about his tennis career. I was curious to see if he'd show any form of excitement when I brought up something positive in his life. It was important to observe his body language, attention span, memory, and thought processes so I could better evaluate his mental health. I wasn't looking for anything particular, but how someone speaks—the whole behavioral element of conversation—that's equally important to the words they choose. You have to pay attention to the full display.

"I think I just had a knack for it," he replied, immediately growing animated. "I was ranked forty-fourth in the United States for players eighteen and under. Lyle's really good, too. We played together a lot and pushed each other to be better. I think that helped with some of the tournaments we went to. We were really competitive."

"Was that the only sport you played competitively?" I asked.

"Some soccer and swimming," he replied. "Not as seriously, though. Tennis just clicked. Lyle even played at Princeton his freshman year. He was probably one of their better players right from the start."

For the next two hours, our conversation followed a similar pattern: a relaxed volley of back-and-forth discussion. We talked about high school, travel, sports, and the differences between the east coast and LA. For the most part, Erik was thoughtful, polite, and soft-spoken. But there were definitely moments when he showed signs of bravado, too. Especially when he talked about tennis. It seemed freeing for him, almost as if he were back on the court itself—a calmness of instinct unburdened by thought.

Tennis, I remember thinking to myself. *That's his anchor. That's the psychological safety net I can use if his trauma gets pushed too far.*

Since it was just the first conversation of what I assumed would be many, I didn't mention the shooting. More than anything, I wanted him to feel comfortable, to trust me. This meeting would serve as the foundation for harder discussions that would inevitably follow. The biggest challenge was keeping his focus on himself—and away from Lyle. Time and again, Erik found ways to bring up his brother, either directly or by answering questions with an inclusive "we." The two of them clearly had a strong bond.

Then the visiting bell rang. Our time was up.

"This has all been very helpful," I told him. "If it's all right with you, I'll come back and visit you again tomorrow. I'd like to spend that time talking about the night of the shooting."

Erik didn't say anything, just gave a slight nod of acknowledgment.

I looked across the table at him and didn't see a cold-blooded killer. I'd worked with juvenile killers in New York prisons, and Erik didn't fit that mold. He was different. He wasn't aloof or defensive. He wasn't proud of what he did or angry for being asked about it. And he certainly didn't have what prison guards commonly refer to as "attitude." He was mostly just sad and a little bit distant. That was about it.

See, there's a line people cross when they commit something horrific. It changes them. They internalize it and reflect it back to the world—"attitude," as the prison guards call it, or that unsettling sensation people describe as "something just felt off." But Erik had none of that. He was different.

This case was something new.

———————

When the guards escorted Erik into our meeting room the next day, I asked them to uncuff his hands.

"You can keep his legs chained if you have to," I said, "but his hands need to be free."

Neither guard seemed sure what to do. So I pointed to the sheets of paper and colored pencils I'd placed on the table in front of me.

"It's a simple drawing exercise," I explained. "The two of us will be fine. But I appreciate your concern." Then, without giving them a chance to protest, I turned to Erik and asked if he was ready to begin.

He nodded.

"Great. I'd like to start this morning with an interview technique I sometimes use to help people express themselves without having to rely on words. I'd like you to draw some of the memories you have of the events that happened in the days leading up to the shooting. It can be anything at all—just draw whatever comes to mind. Does that sound okay?"

"Sure." Erik hesitated. "But I'm not much of an artist."

"That's fine," I reassured him. "There's no style points for this. You can add symbols and words, too, if that's helpful. The exercise is just a way for you to focus on your memories. There's no right or wrong. You can draw them any way you like."

After reaching for a blank piece of paper and a red pencil, Erik began to draw a series of lines on the top half of the page. He paused for a moment, but I didn't say anything. The whole point of the drawings was that they were a nonleading way of gathering information. Think of them like a mini-Rorschach test, in a sense—helpful for me in how they bypassed certain filters and limits of language, and helpful for him in how he could put certain thoughts on paper that were too hard to express in words.

Erik looked at me and took a breath. He regripped the pencil, then scribbled two chairs and a table. Sitting on the chair to the left, he drew a large red stick figure with a frowning face, labeled "Dad." On the chair to the right, he drew himself, much smaller than his father.

"This was when Dad and I had a conversation about college," he clarified, concentrating on his drawing.

Beneath the figure labeled "Dad," Erik wrote in all caps:

"YOU'RE GOING TO TAKE THIS COURSE AND THIS COURSE. I WANT YOU HOME DURING THE WEEK TO STUDY AND SLEEP HERE. THE WORK YOU WILL TAKE WE CAN DO TOGETHER. YOU'RE NOT GOING TO WASTE YOUR TIME TAKING A STUPID DRAMA CLASS. COLLEGE IS HARD WORK. YOU'RE GOING TO STUDY, PAL, AND THAT'S FINAL."

Below that, in a thought bubble coming from the smaller stick figure, Erik wrote: "No dad has this all planned out. I'm not going to be able to get away. He wants to be in charge of my college life. He wants me to come home often during the week to sleep here. To work with him he won't leave me alone! Get away already!!"

And then, beneath the thought bubble, Erik transcribed a verbal response to the other figure: "But Dad, what about the drama class I wanted to take? Don't I have time for that?"

"That's very good," I said. "Did your mother feel the same way about you going to college?"

Erik took a new piece of paper and used the same red pencil to draw a line across the page lengthwise. Above the line, he drew a small red stick figure (labeled "E") as well as a red desk, red windows, and a red bed. He then switched to an orange pencil to add in some squiggly lined circles on the bed, and a blue pencil to draw a large blue stick figure labeled "Mom," who was holding more of the same squiggly lined circles in her hands.

"What are those?" I inquired.

"Clothes," Erik replied. "Mom would always complain about having to pick up after us all the time."

He then added a label of "E-bedroom" to the picture and filled in the bottom half of the page with narration. Under the stick figure of himself, he scribbled: "I don't want to be here anymore I don't care. I just want to go. I can work. I can do things. You just never let me."

Under the figure of his mom, he wrote: "You're not going anywhere. What do you think you're going to do? Work? HAHA. You've never worked a day in your life. You don't know how to do anything. You can't just survive without us baby feeding you. Who do you think you are, YOU STUPID IDIOT! You're not going anywhere! Don't talk back to me!"

Now, immersed in the activity, Erik grabbed a new sheet of paper and started working on a third picture that expanded upon the same theme. The setting and background were almost identical to the composition before it, but the mom had been replaced by the dad—a large and imposing figure with a blue frown and red eyes. Erik drew himself smaller in this picture, cornered by a window, as his father stood close to him. He also added black cloud-like lines across most of the room.

Under the figure of himself, he wrote: "Ahh, I'm not going anywhere. I promise I'll be here. I'll be here."

Then, under the figure of his father, written in all caps: "Just what do you think you're doing, you son of a bitch! Listen to me; *you're not going anywhere.* I thought I told you that before. You can't get away. I'm leaving tomorrow. You had better be here when I get back! You understand me? I'll find you. Believe it. We're going to deal with this when I get back and so help me, God, it's going to be 10 times worse if I find you gone, you son of a bitch!"

A fourth drawing depicted Erik watching a confrontation between his mom and his brother. A small blue stick figure of Lyle was begging his mom to give him back his toupee: "Please, Mom! I really need it. PLEASE don't do this to me." The mother responded: "You don't need it. Your not going to have it and that's final. Stop arguing with me. Well, you pay for it on your own if you want it. Its not my fault you needed it."

Erik had placed himself off to a corner in this picture, with a thought bubble over his head that said: "Wow. I don't believe this. Lyle, just be quiet and don't say anything. She is going crazy."

One of the most notable things about these illustrations was that Erik continued to draw himself smaller and smaller from one picture to the next. This likely conveyed his fear, the fact that he wanted to stay undetectable and hidden away. And the use of cloud-like black streaks in the second and third drawings were significant, too, showing how trapped Erik felt by his father.

"The figures are very expressive," I noted. "And the words you're including are helpful. I'm wondering if you could draw a picture that shows how you felt about your family in the days before the shooting. Can you do that?"

Erik paused for a moment before taking a new sheet of paper. He then used a red pencil to write "Lyle's guesthouse" and "Tues" in the top right corner. Still using red, he drew the inside of the house, then a stick figure representing Lyle and a stick figure representing himself. Next to himself, he wrote: "I want us to be close. The family is falling apart. I don't want to lose you...Remember things happened between Dad and I? A long time ago? They're still happening. Sex things. I'm sorry sorry. I didn't want it to happen. Wanted it to stop."

Above the stick figure of Lyle, he added: "You mean it's been going on all this time! Still? Did you enjoy it?! Didn't you tell anyone why? Didn't you try to stop it?! Does Mom know? THIS IS NEVER GOING TO HAPPEN AGAIN, little brother. He's NEVER going to touch you AGAIN!"

Erik's pace was picking up speed, increasingly frenetic. The next five drawings were all labeled "Thursday." The first of these was like a single-panel comic strip, where blue lines mapped out the progress as a stick figure labeled "Dad" chased a small stick figure labeled "E," threw "E" on a bed, and raped him while smiling with a big black grin.

The words read: "You son of a bitch. I told you never to tell Lyle. EVER. I *warned* you. But you didn't listen. Now he's going to go tell everybody, you son of a bitch, and I can't let that happen."

The small stick figure of Erik responded with: "No, he's not going to tell anyone. I swear. He's not going to tell anyone."

The next two drawings continued the story of what had happened that Thursday. Erik was now focused more on writing out words from a conversation he remembered having with his mom than he was on drawing the two rudimentary stick figures of them in red and black.

Erik: "Oh, you don't understand."
Mom: "What wrong with you?" (smirk) "Oh, I understand. I understand more than you think. I've always known."

Erik: "WHAT? YOU KNOW?! What do you mean you know?! Why didn't you do anything? I HATE YOU."

Mom: "What, do you think I'm stupid? HA. You're the idiot. I understand things between you and dad."

Erik: "I HATE YOU."

This dialogue flowed over into the next drawing, which depicted Erik's mom chasing him through the house.

Mom: "Get back here, you bastard! Don't you ever say that to me, you bastard!"

Erik: "I HATE YOU! I *HATE* YOU!"

The next two pictures skipped ahead to later that Thursday night, with Lyle and a much smaller Erik deep in conversation in Lyle's guest house. Neither stick figure had arms or any facial features, and the drawing was dominated by thick zigzags of black.

Erik: "Lyle, she *knows*."

Lyle: "Why didn't you ever do anything? Why didn't you ever stop that asshole?"

As their mom enters through a door, she starts screaming: "Don't tell me what to do! Nobody ever helped me; why should I help you? *Nobody* ever did anything for me. All you are...are problems. *Your* the cause of all my problems."

The next drawing shows the same scene but without the mother. The stick figures of Erik and Lyle have arms now, but still no facial features, which could suggest the degree of emotional detachment the brothers felt from their mom.

> **Erik:** "You threatened Dad! Are you crazy? What have you done?! He's going to kill us. For sure. Oh my god, I don't believe this. We're goners. It's over."
>
> **Lyle:** "Just calm down. Please, Erik—calm down. Don't panic. I'm scared, too, but we need to be calm, if we're going to live. *STOP IT.* God, Erik, we need to think of something."

At this point in the session, Erik was wholly focused on these drawings, almost as if I wasn't even in the room with him. He raced from one picture to the next without needing any of my prompts, while I silently let him process the events for himself.

"Fri night," he scribbled down on a new sheet of paper. Picking up the blue pencil now, he depicted two small stick figures—labeled "E" and "Lyle"—and one larger stick figure labeled "Mom." Then he filled in almost the entire background with thick streaks of black.

> **Mom:** "The fishing trip has been changed to tomorrow night...I don't know, because that is just the way it is. I forgot to tell you the time had changed."
>
> **Erik and Lyle:** "What? Why? Who goes shark fishing at night? Are you sure? Why are you just changing it? Why? This is *weird.* Why at night?"

The next picture featured a bird's-eye view of the Saturday night fishing trip for sharks. Erik drew himself and his brother hiding at the bow of the boat, whispering to each other: "Can you see them? What are they doing?" He added in his mom and dad at the back of the boat, throwing chum into bloody red water as bait.

In the next picture, the family had returned to their house after the evening fishing trip. A stick figure labeled "Dad" was now banging on Erik's door: "Open this goddamn door. I *know* you're in there. Open this *fucking door*, open it *now*...You can't stay in there forever. You'll *have* to come out tomorrow and I'll be waiting."

In a thought bubble above his own head, Erik scribbled: "Please, God, don't let him in. Please, God, make him go away. Do I shoot him? Or do I run away now? What about Mom? She'll kill me. I only have two shots. Oh no, oh please, God...make him go away. Two shots aren't enough. Do I run now??"

At this point, I noticed Erik slowing down a bit, picking up a lighter color palette and taking his time to draw the outside of a church: an orange-and-yellow cross, green streaks of grass, a bubbling blue fountain. He placed himself outside the building and looking at the door, with a thought bubble that said: "Please, Lord, tell me what to do. I'm afraid. I don't want to die. But I'm tired. I can't go on. Please, Lord, *tell me what to do*. I'm afraid to go inside, Lord. I hope you understand."

I could tell we'd reached a pivotal point in the story, and I wanted him to keep going.

"What happened that night?" I prompted, encouraging him to continue.

He paused for a moment and then slid the church drawing

off to the side, picking up another sheet of paper from the stack. Then he drew black lines and arrows that represented movement through a crude floor plan of the family home. Interestingly, there were no stick figures in this particular scene. It was an intentional omission, I felt, given that the previous dozen pictures were covered with stick figures—and I thought it could possibly suggest denial or avoidance. In place of figures and bubbles, there was a simple label that read: "Lyle + Erik entering the house 7:45."

The next picture was pure chaos, featuring Erik and Lyle as two very small stick figures. Lyle was standing close to a much larger stick figure labeled "Dad," and the words beneath him read: "I'm not going to let you touch my little brother . . . *ever* . . . *again.*"

For the first time in the series, the dad stick figure was drawn using the same color as the boys, which could be suggestive of a merging between the victim and the offender, and he was saying: "Don't you tell me what to do. *I* say what goes on in this family. Erik, go up to your room; I'll be there in a few minutes. I said go *now!*"

After drawing red streaks coming out of his dad's face, Erik put down the pencil, and—almost as if in a trance—he positioned his hands as if he was holding a shotgun, and slowly made a firing motion, reenacting what had happened next. It wasn't clear if the movement was meant for me or himself. He didn't look at me. He simply stared at the stick figures of his dad and his mom, slowly nodding his head.

A moment later, he drew the same scene again on another piece of paper. This version, however, was significantly calmer, with fewer black lines cluttering the space. He drew a body that appeared to be his father, scribbled over as if to show that he was dead. Lastly, he added in himself and Lyle—both of them a little bigger in this version—with Lyle confronting a stick figure of their mom.

Lyle: "Why can't we go out? We're not going out? Why not? Why can't we? Why do you want us to stay?"

Mom: "You can't go out. You're not going to leave this house. Because . . . because . . . *AHHH*. Because I *said* you're not."

When Erik eventually put down the pencil, he looked exhausted, as if he'd exorcised the entire memory from his consciousness.

"It's not easy," I murmured, saying this not to comfort him, but because it was true.

But I doubt he even heard me.

Trauma is like that. It's a whole self-contained world. If you open up to it, if you slip beneath its waters, there's no simple way of coming back up for air. Erik was somewhere beneath those murky waters now.

"All right. Let's call it a day, then." I stood up. "These drawings have been very helpful."

He winced slightly, but that was his sum response.

I tapped on the door and signaled to the guards that we were finished. After making sure that Erik's cuffs were secure, they led him away, and I was left to ponder everything that had just transpired.

Leslie was right, I thought to myself. It was clear to me that there was *much* more to this case than anyone realized. It wasn't just about wealthy teens acting out against their parents, or even trying to inherit a big sum. Instead, there was a deeply complex history of tension, trauma, and violence that had led directly to the events of that late August evening. And if the jury was going to decide a fair punishment to fit this crime, it was absolutely crucial for them to understand and factor in this context, too.

CHAPTER 3

Prison Interlude

As fascinating as these interview sessions with Erik were, not all of them went exactly according to plan. For example, at one of our first scheduled interviews, I showed up to the prison at our agreed-upon time, identified myself to the guard, and was told, "Sorry, no visitors," in a voice absent of any tone.

"What do you mean, no visitors?" I pushed back.

But a quick look at the linebacker-sized man standing across from me and I could tell I wouldn't get an explanation. He knew the rights of inmates as well as I did. *No visitors* meant "no explanation required." That's the nature of correctional facilities. They're complex and labyrinthine and rigidly adherent to their own organizing principles—not a whole lot of traffic between what comes out and what goes in.

It took some time, but I eventually got the knack for navigating prison systems and their accompanying idiosyncrasies. I didn't really have a choice in the matter. Whether it's prisons specifically or government red tape or simply the legal system itself, bureaucracy is just part of the job, and that includes the occasional inmate cancellation or delay, like what had happened with Erik. And it makes sense, if you think about it. For one thing, prisoners have rights, too. For example, they might get sick and have that information protected by the same Health Insurance Portability and Accountability Act as the rest of us. Unfortunately, it also means that you can't call ahead of time to confirm whether or not a visit is still on. You just have to show up. And when you do, there's always a slim but very real chance you'll be given a stern look, told to take a seat, and find yourself in a bureaucratic purgatory of sorts, waiting for all the moving parts to line up so that you can actually meet the person you're there to see. It might last minutes, hours, or the entire day. All you can do is try to make the most of it.

The upside of all this waiting around was that the prison guards tended to be just as bored as I was. They couldn't help but gravitate toward time-passing distractions. Maybe not at first. But as soon as I mentioned my research at the FBI and the types of cases in which I was testifying, the guards tended to perk up and start sharing stories of their own. Their insights were like cutting through a mile of red tape. They pulled back the curtain to share firsthand knowledge about prison behaviors, day-to-day dynamics, and the ever-shifting social structures taking place within their facilities. It was fascinating. And what it taught me was that, even after an offender's been convicted of a crime and placed within the highly structured environment of a prison's reinforced walls, they still find ways to manifest their core behaviors. They still adhere to a continuity of self that prison can't easily erase. This was something I could use to my advantage, I realized.

By tapping into the predictive aspect of an inmate's behavior, I could better unlock the secrets within their head to more wholly understand them.

One example came at the start of the 1980s. This was early on in my trial work, back when I was still focused primarily on developing the criminal profiling methodology for the FBI's Behavioral Science Unit and only just starting to gain a reputation as a testifying expert for cases of sexual violence. The case itself was fairly typical for the time; it was an assault that took place behind a local bar. But it stood out because of a guard I talked with during my time at the courthouse. He'd bounced around a lot and had worked at San Quentin State Prison during the same time that convicted cult leader Charles Manson was imprisoned there.

"What was he like?" I asked.

"A prick and a showboat. Completely full of himself," the guard said, launching into an expletive-heavy description of how Manson liked to stir up trouble with other prisoners.

I nodded encouragingly, unsurprised until the guard added in a throwaway detail.

"And he had a weird habit of sitting on top of tables whenever visitors came to see him. He'd perch right up there with a big, stupid grin."

That caught my attention. It was so singularly specific. So defining. It was exactly the type of behavior that typified Manson's obsessive need for control. Because of *course* he would choose an elevated position, literally placing himself *above* whomever he was talking to. It would feed into his authoritative sense of self. It would allow him to feel dominant.

"Typical Manson," I murmured, wrapping the conversation up.

During my next visit to Quantico, where I was consulting on several projects for the FBI's Behavioral Science Unit, I shared the Manson insights with Agents Robert Ressler and John Douglas. They agreed this need to maintain dominance was worth exploring. And when they had an opportunity to interview Manson, they made sure to stage the room with a table for Manson to perch himself on top. Which he did, of course. Interestingly, by allowing Manson to gain this supposed "leverage," Ressler was able to get Manson to lower his guard just a bit—and it was at this point that Manson started opening up, saying: "Look Mr. Ressler. If you look deeply into my mind, you're going to see your own reflection."

Another example led to new insight on John Wayne Gacy, "the Killer Clown," a serial offender who raped, tortured, and murdered dozens of boys and young men for over a six-year period in the suburbs of Chicago, Illinois, in the mid-1970s. Like many narcissists, Gacy craved admiration, remaining obsessed with his public image even years after he'd been locked behind bars. But Gacy's obsession went a step further than his peers. He went so far as to design and produce his own prison stationery to correspond with journalists, law enforcement, and fans. The stationery included bloodred lettering with all-caps text that read, "JUST A NOTE FROM JOHN WAYNE GACY," alongside an equally bloodred drawing of a skeletal clown.

He sent a few of these letters to the BSU while I was there. And honestly, my first impression was that they must be a joke. They were just so desperate. So cartoony. But Gacy saw the whole thing in a different light. In his mind, where his truest self existed as the lived fantasy of Pogo the Killer Clown, his actions were a form of idolatry. The image he'd so meticulously crafted was what he cared about most—and branded stationery was a crude means of forcing that image to endure.

The doldrums of prison bureaucracy presented other opportunities to gain insights, too. One of these was learning to navigate the rudimentary prison email systems. I corresponded with Montie Rissell this way. He was a serial rapist in the mid-1970s whose crimes grew increasingly brutal and frequent until they escalated to murder. I didn't understand much about escalation at the time, and I was curious to see if Rissell recognized the cause of his own escalation. I also wanted to know if he thought the police could have done anything differently to speed up their investigation.

After I reached out to him, he wrote back the following message:

Hello! I was just now finally able to check my emails and saw your name on my account now. I am responding to let you know that right now is not a good time for us to get together to discuss the issues you wanted to get to talk about...I am still willing to discuss and share any thoughts or outlooks I may have towards what you want to ask or know in the future. As I outlined before I think some form of compensation is in order but, as you know, the Son of Sam law prevents ME from receiving it personally but, it doesn't stop you from compensating my wife or brother for it providing they are providing something in a technical or advisory participation.

Let me know what your thoughts are on this and we'll go from there...Once we work out these details, I am willing to answer and help in any way possible when it is feasible. Until then take care.

Yours Truly,

Montie Rissell

I wasn't surprised that Rissell wanted compensation. But I certainly wasn't going to accommodate that request. It was telling, though, that even years after his crimes, his focus still came back to me, me, "ME."

Before long, inmates started initiating contact with me rather than waiting to see if I'd reach out to them. These offenders were typically older, had been incarcerated longer, and had gotten to a point of self-reflection where they wanted to understand the underlying reason for what they'd done. For the most part, they were trying to reconcile who they were, and they hoped that I could provide a simple answer for them.

Occasionally, however, I received strange requests that felt somehow "off" or "wrong." One of these came from Duane Samples, a horrific murderer who acted out his fantasy of raping and dismembering beautiful women—and who also fetishized the idea of being a victim of dismemberment himself, once writing to a woman that he wanted her to "eviscerate and emasculate me." His letter was polite enough, just a simple greeting followed by his prison address and a request that I send him reprints of the journal articles I'd written on murder and mutilation. I considered it, but decided not to respond. The absence of emotion, combined with the coolness of the request—it struck me as less about finding answers and more about dipping into the violence of the past.

No way, I thought. *I won't indulge him.*

All these case studies in the behavioral analysis of convicted offenders were fascinating, each one worthy of pursuit in its own right. But as an expert witness, the real value of this analysis, for me, came down to one crucial factor—sentencing.

In criminal court cases, part of my role is to develop a Pre-sentencing Report that includes a summary of any infractions and disciplinary actions that the defendant incurred during their incarceration. This report provides judges with relevant context for their sentencing decisions in the future. One of the most significant considerations when sentencing a violent offender is assessing the potential danger they might pose if or when they're released back into society. By knowing what an offender's infractions were, and then comparing these to a baseline of infractions committed by other offenders, I was able to help contextualize these infractions and clarify the underlying psychology behind them, which ultimately aided judges in making fair and better informed decisions.

I spent a lot of time thinking about these things on my drive from the prison to Leslie Abramson's house in LA. Sentencing, for Erik and Lyle, was all they had left. They'd already admitted to killing their parents in a step-by-step confession that rendered their actions perfectly clear. And it was clear, too, that they'd been vilified and deemed guilty in the court of public opinion. But those things were beyond my control.

All I could do was make sure Erik and Lyle received sentencing based on the full circumstances of their case—not just the crime, but the complex reality that had led them to that moment.

CHAPTER 4

The Menendez Trial

Preexisting cultural beliefs are more ingrained into our psyche than we realize. That's just the nature of living in a society: We rely on a shared framework of rules and expectations to provide an organizing structure within the chaos of day-to-day existence. But while it's comforting to know we all operate within this same framework, it doesn't mean our beliefs are always justified. Or even right.

Let's do an exercise. Close your eyes for a moment and picture a victim of a violent sexual assault. What does that person look like? Are they male or female? Old or young? Attractive or plain?

More often than not, the word "victim" conjures up an abstract ideal of an innocent young, attractive woman in the wrong place at the wrong time. This prevailing cultural expectation is reinforced by the fictionalized victims in shows like *Law & Order*, *Criminal Minds*, and on and on. And that's all fine and entertaining on the surface. But the problem is that this expectation carries over into real life. And so, whenever a victim *doesn't* fit this standard, it challenges the very framework we've come to expect—and that's not easy for us to overcome.

In the case of Erik and Lyle Menendez, they were nearly an exact inverse from the typical societal expectation of what a victim looked and acted like. They knew no one would believe them if they dared to come forward. Their abuser knew this, too—and this created a perfect scenario for their victimization to fester and continue over an extended period of time. Add to this the fact that they were being abused by their own father—a highly regarded entertainment executive—and it's easy to see why they felt hopeless. It must've seemed like they had nowhere to turn to. No one they could trust.

"What we're talking about, this strategy of an imperfect self-defense, it's going to be a bombshell," Leslie said, sitting across from me in her kitchen. "I've seen a few cases where the defense centered around a murderer's history of trauma and fear, but those were typically in cases where women killed their abusive husbands. We'll be the first to use this approach for a male defendant, let alone two."

"It shouldn't matter," I insisted. "They were only boys when their father started abusing them. Their story's credible. And Erik's drawings will back up their testimony, too."

"We can't use the drawings in court. They'd be inadmissible hearsay if offered for the truth of the representations. And with Erik testifying, they'd be too childlike to avoid withering cross-examination."

"So it's their word versus the perfect reputation of their father?"

"I know, I know." Leslie sighed. "It's going to be a real challenge to get the jury on our side. Their initial impression of Erik and Lyle will be that the brothers are two grown men, born into a life of privilege and over-the-top Hollywood luxury, with *millions* of dollars at stake. Perception is everything. Remember, these two grew up in what seemed like a perfect family, with the world at their fingertips—and that type of story is a *lot* easier to sell a jury than the reality of male-on-male sexual abuse."

"That's all the more reason why we should focus on the child-development aspect of this case," I maintained. "The psychology is clear. Erik's drawings and interviews are fully consistent with today's standards of research on abuse. I can explain that to the jury, how two boys would be so fundamentally damaged that they'd kill the parents who raised them."

"That's another point we have to be careful about," Leslie reminded me. "The prosecution will be focused solely on the present. They'll make a concerted effort to dismiss Erik and Lyle's past so that the jury will only think about *their* actions, without necessarily taking into consideration all of the actions that were done *to* them. If we want to get ahead of that narrative, we need to lay out a clear timeline, going all the way back to the boys' childhood. We need the jury to think about *why* these two did what they did, to emphasize that they were responding to all of the cruelty that had been inflicted upon them leading up to the time of the murders."

"The child-development angle will help a lot in this regard," I agreed. "A key motive for this extreme form of self-defense was that there was this history of fear and abuse, one that fostered a genuine belief that their parents were going to kill them. Murder was their response to—"

"Careful not to call it 'murder,'" Leslie interrupted me. "That's important. They *did* shoot and kill their parents. But we're not doing ourselves any favors by calling it 'murder.' 'Shootings'—that's our term. That's the difference between murder and imperfect self-defense."

"Right." I hesitated. "Why 'shooting' was their response to the trauma they'd endured over the years. I think it's important to acknowledge that the boys are responsible for what they did, but, to your point, we need to show that everything leading up to the shootings is what caused them to pull the trigger. Whatever consequences they face, all of this context needs to be taken into account."

"It's a risky approach," Leslie said. "I'm not sure the country is ready to talk about male-on-male abuse."

"Maybe not," I said. "But that's the reality of the situation, regardless of cultural norms. Plus, culture is *always* resistant to change."

Leslie nodded. "There's one other thing we need to be clear on," she said, looking me square in the eyes. "I brought you into this because your credentials are so unique. You worked with the FBI, you have psychological skills and legal experience, and you don't ever seem to get tripped up. And on top of all that, you're a nurse. What I'm trying to say here is that your résumé is very impressive. But I also know how the prosecution is going to play it. They're going to do everything they can to strip you of all your accolades. They'll not so subtly focus on the fact that you're a woman, dismissing you as emotional and unreliable. Trust me, I've been dealing with it my entire career."

"Unfortunately, so have I," I said, recalling all the times I'd been underestimated by this type of reductive thinking before.

There was almost a bit of irony to the situation. A female attorney. A female expert witness. And two boys who were victims of sexual assault.

"Good." She seemed a bit more relieved. "So you'll understand that since I get to question you first, I'm going to build you up and take that line of attack away from them. I'll ask about your research, academics, law enforcement experience, criminology, and everything else you're an expert in. They can do their best to tear you down, but it'll be impossible for them to deny everything you've done. Just...just don't let them get under your skin. We can't risk any surprises up there."

That last part stung. I appreciated Leslie's directness—I knew she was trying to be helpful, and I valued the fact that she trusted me enough to speak honestly—but it was also a stark reminder of the uphill battle we were about to face.

This was a capital case.

The stakes were life or death.

———

"The defense calls Dr. Ann Burgess."

I approached the witness stand in a courtroom in the Los Angeles County Courthouse on October 19, 1993, raised my left hand over the Bible, and was solemnly sworn in before taking my seat. In front of me, what seemed like endless rows of media and spectators were jam-packed elbow to elbow. Several TV cameras reoriented in my direction. I searched for Leslie Abramson's face, smiled, and took a deep breath.

I knew the process—I'd testified dozens of times over the years and seen the very real impact on people's lives. But this trial was different. Its scale set it apart. The Menendez brothers' case had ballooned into a larger-than-life idea, standing out even among all the glitz and glamour of Beverly Hills. The public was totally captivated by their story, drawn to its theatrical twists—family secrets, lavish spending, and allegations of incestuous abuse. Enthralled, spectators lined up outside the courthouse in the pre-dawn hours, eager for the chance to sit inside and bear witness.

I didn't envy Leslie's job here, but she seemed to take it all in stride. She dominated the courtroom with all the command of a seasoned actress. She even looked the part—with sharply tailored suits, a puff of golden hair, and a flair for dramatic mannerisms and eye rolls that prompted Judge Stanley M. Weisberg to ask: "Are you inviting the court to find you in contempt?"

"No, no," Leslie had responded. "I'm only saying there's only so much unfairness one can bear."

Her verbal jousting was enthralling. She accused Weisberg of being "biased," constantly interrupting him. And for the first few days of the trial, I watched from the sidelines, taking it all in. But now it was my turn to present the jury with the information they needed to fairly assess the crime. I took a deep breath and looked up to meet Leslie's gaze.

After a long preamble about my credentials, background, academics, and professional experience, Leslie cut to the chase.

I was ready.

"You mentioned," Leslie began, "that you've been collecting research throughout your career, and that your early research involved understanding victims of rape. Can you tell me: Are you familiar with the term 'rape trauma syndrome'?"

"Yes," I said, nodding. "I am."

"And where did that term come from?"

"That was a term I coined with a colleague of mine years ago, based on our research working with victims of sexual abuse." I explained how trauma is both a physical and emotional response to sexual abuse, and that it sometimes manifests in ways that are beyond the scope of an individual's typical behaviors. "We published all of this research in the *American Journal of Psychiatry* in 1974."

"Has that concept, that syndrome you defined, has it been accepted by both the law enforcement and psychiatric communities?"

"Yes, it has."

"And as a consequence of your research and writing in this area, and with your subsequent recognition as an expert in sexual abuse, were you contacted by the Federal Bureau of Investigation?"

"Yes, I was."

I could see where Leslie was heading with this line of questioning. She knew that the jury would have a difficult time accepting the brothers' account of the childhood abuse they'd endured. So she built up toward the inevitable slowly and decisively, shining a light not just on my own expertise, but on the taboos surrounding domestic abuse that could prevent victims from speaking out initially. Essentially, she needed the jury to respect that the problem was *real* before bringing up Erik and Lyle's traumatic history in the home.

"And what was your role with the FBI? What were you helping the agency accomplish?" Leslie continued.

"At that particular time," I replied, "the FBI Academy, which was responsible for training agents as well as other law enforcement

officers, had received a congressional mandate to provide training around rape and sexual assault. But before they could develop
their training materials, they needed more information about
victims—about how and why offenders choose their victims.
I was brought in because of my expertise in victimology, and
because I'd already been working with victims directly to better
understand their role in the investigative process. Essentially, I
helped the FBI in developing those types of training materials,
but I was also working with agents in a research capacity: making sense of the data they were collecting through interviews with
perpetrators of sex crimes, while also developing a protocol for
more effectively interviewing perpetrators of sex crimes so that
we could use this information to find patterns and predictors in
suspect apprehension in the future."

"So you were trying to find similar patterns within perpetrators of these types of crimes to assist law enforcement in appre-
hending other perpetrators of similar crimes?" Leslie clarified.

I nodded. "Yes."

"What other projects have you been involved in during your
affiliation with the FBI?"

"For the past ten years, I've also been involved in a study called
the Crime Classification project. My role has been to look at how
investigators examine crime scenes, the types of records, photographs, information, forensics—the massive amount of information they have to account for—and essentially their whole process
of how they come to an investigative decision about the material
they've seen. That information, that data, has become the basis for
how we define different categories of crimes."

"Now, according to the FBI guidelines, there are thirty-two

categories of homicides, correct? And is one of them known as 'domestic homicide,' which is defined by some type of relationship between the victim and the offender?"

There was a subtle shift in this new line of questioning—one that would've been easy to miss if I hadn't been expecting it. Now that my clinical expertise had been established, Leslie was no longer trying to reinforce its existence. She was now moving forward as if this expertise was a given. It was a simple persuasion technique known as the authority principle, basically an appeal to someone's tendency to comply or agree with individuals in perceived positions of authority. In the eyes of the jury, Leslie—as the Menendez brothers' primary attorney—was a figure of authority in the courtroom. And so, by speaking to me as a fellow figure of authority—an expert on forensics—my credibility grew in the eyes of the jury, too.

"Let's focus on this particular case," Leslie continued. "By applying guidelines from the FBI crime classification methodology to this specific crime scene, are you able to make some assessments about the crime scene?"

"Yes. The crime scene analysis indicates that this was a domestic killing, meaning that the killing happened in the context of an intimate or familial relationship. There's no forced entry, and there's no evidence of material being taken, of theft. Plus, the bodies were not touched or moved, meaning the death scene was the same as the crime scene. All of those aspects tend to indicate that there's a known relationship between the victims and their attackers, that these people are not strangers to one another."

"Now, you were telling us earlier about the classifications of a crime scene. Why would the FBI, or any law enforcement agency for example, want to…what investigative purpose does it serve to analyze a crime scene to see if there has been planning or no planning?"

"Well, it's generally going to tell the investigative officer where to focus their investigation: what type of person, relationship, etc. to be on the lookout for."

"Are there certain crime scenes that reveal a great deal about the perpetrator? If not their actual identity, at least some defining personality characteristics? And with respect to those kinds of crime scenes, can a great deal be learned from the psychology, if you will, of the perpetrator?"

"Yes," I confirmed. "In fact, that's essentially what the FBI would describe it as. When they look at a crime scene, they're trying to figure out the 'personality,' if you will, of the crime itself. And don't forget that the other part of the study is the interview component. Agents interviewed these persons—people who had been convicted of serial crimes—and talked to them about their crimes. So the research that went into understanding offender psychology, that didn't just come from the crime scenes; it also came from direct conversations with offenders who talked about their crimes at great length."

"Now, your experience includes assisting the FBI to name and describe the three main classifications of a crime scene: organized, disorganized, or mixed. Applying these guidelines and analytical methods to the crime scene here, what conclusion did you reach about what kind of crime scene this was?"

"I will preface this by saying that there generally may be indicators of both organized and disorganized elements within a single crime scene," I replied. I knew my answer here—and the specific wording I used—would be critical. "But within this crime scene, I saw more elements of disorganization."

"Under the FBI's criteria, what was disorganized about this crime scene?"

"Location is the first thing to pay attention to here. This crime occurred in a residential area, and those kinds of areas are generally quieter. The weapon used to kill Mr. and Mrs. Menendez was a shotgun, and there were a number of shots fired, which would've been very noisy and would've attracted attention. It's also important to consider injuries to victims, both the number of them and where they are on the body. An organized offender would use a minimal number of shots to accomplish the task. In this case, though, the number of shots was excessive, which speaks to a disorganized crime scene. And that last point also speaks to the emotionality of the crime, what's sometimes referred to as 'overkill.' Certainly, in this crime scene, far more shots were fired than necessary in order to accomplish the task, which points to a high degree of emotion. And the randomness of all the shots, the lack of concentration on one given part of the victims' bodies—both of those things speak to a more pervasive emotion, rather than a singular feeling of anger or rage. The randomness of all the shots speaks to fear. There was also a lack of staging at this particular crime scene, meaning that the bodies weren't tampered with or moved, which is another indicator of disorganization. We commonly see staging when an offender is trying to cover up the crime or lead the investigation into another direction."

There was a heaviness to the room now. A weight of anticipation hung silently over the jury as everyone looked on. Eyes followed the conversation between me, Leslie, and back to me again. The whole thing felt like slow motion. Like being underwater.

Leslie then went on to ask about all the different types of risks that were present in this specific crime scene, risks that could speak to the disorganization of the offenders. I explained that there was a high risk of detection from the noise, blood splatter, and gunshot residue left behind. I also pointed out the risk of one offender accidently shooting the other, considering the close space and large number of shots fired. There was a postcrime risk, too, in how the offenders removed the shotgun shells from the crime scene—they were basically carrying around evidence *with* them, thus connecting themselves forensically to the crime. All of that contributed to my analysis of this crime as poorly planned, if it had been planned at all.

After establishing the disorganized nature of the crime—and subtly framing her questions to suggest the emotional trauma evident in this specific domestic, highly disorganized crime—Leslie switched tack again, pursuing a line of questions that focused on my experiences working with victims of childhood sexual assault. She'd pinned two diagrams of the human brain to a corkboard behind me, and then asked about the science of brain function as it related to abuse and trauma.

"And what area of research did that work lead you to?" Abramson asked.

This gave me an opportunity to talk about how trauma impacts adolescent brains. I didn't mention Erik or Lyle specifically. That would come later. For now, I was building up the scaffolding, explaining psychological and physiological mechanisms to the jury, and showing them how victims could, in some cases, commit violence as a last resort. I was creating the channels the jury would later need to access the truth.

———

When it came time for the prosecution to approach the witness stand, I was relieved to find their line of questioning as predictable as it was surpassable. Initially, the attorneys tried to discredit my expertise, especially in regard to how it related to the trial. And when that didn't work, they switched tactics and started discrediting Erik and Lyle's trauma. The media had already characterized the brothers as cruel, unsympathetic, spoiled rich kids who were guilty of murder-for-money. So the prosecution merely needed to drive home the narrative that was already out there. When the issue of the boys' sexual abuse came up, the prosecution mocked it. They brought in prominent psychiatrists who knew nothing about sexual assault but who confidently dismissed these issues nonetheless. The most well-known of these was a forensic psychiatrist named Park Dietz, who testified that after fifteen hours of interviews, he'd observed Erik to be overly self-dramatizing and prone to histrionics.

Curiously, while the Menendez brothers trial unfolded in the courtroom, a parallel trial was playing out in the media at the same time. Court TV hired *Playboy* reporter Robert Rand and *Vanity Fair*'s Dominick Dunne to disagree with each other and give opposing weekly rebuttals on camera, with Rand siding with the prosecution and Dunne with the defense. This model of real-time, public-facing expertise debate was a fairly new phenomenon for crime watchers, though a similar model had been used with the ten-day William Kennedy Smith rape trial in 1991, which was nationally publicized due to Smith's familial connection to Senator Ted Kennedy and Representative Patrick J. Kennedy.

What was fascinating to me about the media element was how it shined a spotlight on certain individuals in the case, exposing their nature more completely than the carefully maintained professionalism they brought to the courtroom. In the case of Dunne, before the trial even began, he publicly stated his doubt that José ever molested his sons, telling the camera, "I never believed for a second that he sexually abused them." But after Lyle Menendez's first day of testimony, Dunne started to doubt his preconceptions.

When defense attorney Jill Lansing questioned Lyle on the stand and asked him, "Why did you kill your parents?" Lyle's reply had been heartbreaking.

"Because we were afraid," Lyle whispered, clearly devastated. "He raped me."

> **Lansing:** "Did you cry?"
> **Lyle:** "Yes."
> **Lansing:** "Did you bleed?"
> **Lyle:** "Yes."
> **Lansing:** "Were you scared?"
> **Lyle:** "Very."
> **Lansing:** "Did you ask him not to?"
> **Lyle:** "Yes."
> **Lansing:** "How did you ask him not to?"
> **Lyle:** "I just told him. I don't... I don't..."

Keep in mind: Lyle was only six years old when he was raped for the first time. He later admitted that he'd misinterpreted sex as a male bonding ritual.

Later in his testimony, Lyle revealed that his father also raped Erik and that he, in turn, replicated that sexual abuse by taking his brother into the woods to molest him in a similar manner. At this point in the testimony, Lyle looked away from his lawyer, and, leaning forward on the stand, faced his brother.

"I don't understand why," he cried, the apology tumbling from his lips, "and I'm sorry!"

As emotional as the testimony was for the brothers, it was just as heart-wrenching for several jurors and reporters, who wept right alongside Lyle and Erik.

It was at that moment that Dominick Dunne, looking shaken, turned to a fellow reporter and said, "I wonder if I am wrong. Could I be wrong?"

Out in the courthouse hallway, Dunne repeated his doubts aloud to another reporter, adding, "I can't believe I'm saying this, but I think I believe this. I think he is telling the truth."

Moments later, Dunne sought me out to ask if we could talk. He wanted my opinion, to which I explained that I'd already given my opinion in court.

"Do you *believe* what Lyle just said?" Dunne pressed.

"I have no reason not to," I said calmly. "Do you?"

Dunne mumbled something about the motive for murder being the inheritance payout.

"Come on," I said with a sigh. "At least *pretend* you're thinking about this critically. None of what you heard was rehearsed.

Besides, they had all the money they ever wanted. What more did they need? And if it wasn't for money, what other motive could they have had?"

From day one, my goal as an expert witness in the Menendez brothers' case was to explain to the jury how years of fear, trauma, and abuse could have culminated in murder. I wasn't trying to justify Lyle's or Erik's actions or portray them as sympathetic figures, nor was I trying to vilify their parents. I was simply trying to show that the boys' actions, as illogical as they might seem to an outsider, made sense from a neurobiological perspective.

After all, that's the way trauma works. It pushes people to do things that they wouldn't ordinarily do, especially if and when they feel their lives are in danger. It was clear to me that Erik and Lyle felt so trapped by their parents, so absolutely powerless, that they believed their only means of escape was to kill them. And I backed up this rationale by citing widely accepted research showing that long-term exposure to fear rewires the brains of human trauma victims.

"[Trauma] can have a major impact on executive functions," I testified back in the courtroom. "Some particularly relevant examples to the case at hand include challenges with impulse control, emotional processing, anticipating the consequences of one's actions, and managing behavioral responses and reactions."

To this, I added that trauma, especially childhood trauma, can create a numbing effect between the individual and the world around them. This often exacerbates challenges to executive functions. It allows the traumatized to feel distant from their actions, less accountable. And for children who are continuously engaged in this numbing mechanism, children who can neither fight nor flee, this cycle of vulnerability impacts the development of their brain. It stunts their ability to fully understand their emotions and navigate them in a societally accepted way. This is why they sometimes act out in violence.

Prosecutor Pamela Bozanich dismissed this explanation as "psychobabble," undermining my expertise without so much as bothering to bring in an expert with any specialized trauma training of their own. Even worse, Bozanich dismissed the reality of male sexual trauma in general, saying that "men could not be raped because they lack the necessary equipment to be raped."

Of course, her assessment was absolutely ludicrous, so I didn't take her attacks on me or my opinion personally. But it's a good example of the gender bias that the brothers were facing in their trial. For all the progress we'd made on validating victims of sexual assault since I first started working with them in the early 1970s, it was clear there was a limit to the scope of those we considered victims—and men existed outside of that boundary.

Bozanich and I continued this back-and-forth for what felt like hours. I spoke honestly and stayed within the firm footing of my expertise. But she had no interest in an honest conversation. Her opinion was already formed. Whether she truly believed her opinion or whether she was simply trying to win a case, that part was less clear.

Still, our conversation was eye-opening. I'd gone into the case—perhaps naïvely—assuming that a trial of such national intrigue would still be grounded in a level of judiciary gravitas. But between the live broadcast on Court TV, the scrum of media members jockeying for seats each morning, and the frenzied crowds lined up outside the courthouse doors, it felt like more of a circus than a legal process—and this seemed to impact even the proceedings of the case itself. I noted that the prosecution in particular thrived on the theatrics permeating the courtroom walls. It wasn't just their performative attitude, either; it was the way they structured their *whole argument* around confirmation bias and misinformation to play to the tabloidesque nature of the case.

But Bozanich's closing statement was perhaps the most grandiose of all. She opportunistically used the moment to highlight the morality of a member of her own family: her father. As it turned out, her father had been sexually abused as a child—just like the Menendez brothers—yet had gone on to join the Navy and live a productive life. "For all those children who were severely abused and who became useful members of society, this defense is an offense," she cried.

I knew Bozanich was only doing her job, but watching her was deeply conflicting. On one hand, I was truly relieved that her father's story had a positive ending—a rarity in my line of work. Too often, I find myself facing victims whose fates are far more tragic.

And yet, that's exactly the thing that makes trauma so complicated—a truth that Bozanich left unsaid. Trauma, by its very nature, is a complex condition that affects everyone differently. It can manifest in ways that are emotional, physical, behavioral, cognitive—or even a mix of all four. Its impact can be minimal and completely recoverable, or it can be debilitating and inescapable for the remainder of the victim's life, or it can be a mix of the two, rearing its ugly head when triggers draw it closer to the surface. I'd seen the full spectrum of traumatic responses—which is how I was able to recognize it in Erik and Lyle in the first place.

Even though I felt I'd done my best to explain how the abuse the brothers endured led to such complex trauma, I still wasn't certain whether my expert testimony had resonated with the jury. When the first trial ended in a hung jury (the jurors had been unable to agree on whether the brothers' actions had been the response to years of abuse, and whether or not it had been pre-planned), I took it as a victory—of sorts. I hoped it meant that I'd been able to get through to at least *some* of those jury members. Interestingly enough, the jury's split of six to six (six in favor of a guilty verdict, six in favor of a not guilty verdict) had been clean-cut by gender. The women believed Erik and Lyle. The men did not. But it still felt like progress in acknowledging the existence of male-on-male sexual abuse and its lasting consequences.

The Menendez brothers' retrial began in August 1995. The same official, Judge Stanley Weisberg, was assigned to this second trial as well. But there were few similarities beyond that. More specifically, Judge Weisberg changed the second trial's rules in three key areas: prohibiting cameras in court; limiting the number of witnesses the defense could call to testify about the boys' experiences of abuse at the hands of their father; and, via a last-minute ruling, refusing to allow the imperfect self-defense theory.

To me, it seemed like these decisions were pretty biased and worked more to the prosecution's favor. How could the defense successfully present their case if the judge prohibited further testimony from all fifty-one witnesses who testified about abuse in the first trial?

It was Jon Conte who eventually told me about the verdict in the second trial.

"Guilty," he said. "Convicted of first-degree murder. They've been sentenced to life in prison with no possibility of parole."

I don't remember how the rest of that conversation went with Jon, but I do remember how my thoughts flashed back to a very specific moment from the first trial, when one of the prosecutors had questioned my impartiality.

"Aren't you an advocate for victims?"

I responded that I'm an advocate for science. That my job as an expert witness is to enable the jury to make informed and educated decisions. Because that's what matters.

I advocate for the truth.

CHAPTER 5

Confidence-Style Offenders

Though I had my hands full with teaching and testifying throughout much of the 1990s and early 2000s, I made a habit of continuing to lecture at the FBI Academy in Quantico. I valued hearing the perspectives of the agents. They never sugarcoated anything. They were always curious and smart. And I often used them as a sounding board for ongoing research or whichever court cases I was working on at the time.

That was the shape of things one morning in the late fall of 1995. I was standing in front of the assembled agents, discussing a new case as part of a lecture on victimology and the psychological responses to trauma.

The offender's name was Charlie Scott.

Honestly, even as I spoke, I was still trying to make sense of the details myself. I'd only recently finished reviewing all the materials in preparation to be a testifying expert for the prosecution. The weight of that responsibility sat heavily on my shoulders, as it always did in cases like this.

Scott was a serial rapist with violent tendencies and a knack for deception—nothing new there. But what stood out was his method of attack. Scott was what's known as a confidence-style rapist, which is somewhat unusual and much less known than the typical blitz types or power-assertive types I'd discussed in the past.

After detailing Scott's background and methods to the gathered agents, I turned off the projector and flipped on the overhead lights.

"Okay," I said. "So, to sum things up, that's why someone like Scott presents such difficulties for investigators and the legal system. Confidence-style offenders use their relationship with the victim to justify their attack. It's a tricky variable. Especially in how it causes victims to feel a conflicted sense of responsibility for what happened, which often leads to delayed reporting, self-blame, and sometimes even an absolute certainty the whole thing was their fault. But it's not their fault. That's something you need to remember. And that's why it's so important to establish the nature of the relationship between offender and victim as early in a case as possible. It shows where the boundaries are, which is key because the very definition of a confidence-style rapist is that they fail to adhere to a relationship's previously established bounds."

There was a brief stillness throughout the room, then a shuffling of papers followed by the metallic click of a dozen briefcases clasping shut.

Good, I thought, turning back to the lectern to pack up my notes.

A voice cut through the murmurs of departure.

"That last definition sounded like a typical woman," I overheard one of the agents say. "I've known a few of them myself. They'll flirt with you and lead you on, then they'll blame you when they regret it the next morning."

"Excuse me?" I asked, stopping the entire room dead in its tracks. "Is there something you wanted to discuss?"

"No, no." The agent looked at me wide-eyed. "I was just... talking. That's all."

He stared at his shoes and waited for whatever would come next.

But nothing did come next. Not because I didn't *want* to berate this man for missing the obvious point. Trust me, I did. Every fiber in my being *wanted* to explain how the whole crux of the Scott case revolved around stigma and bias and exactly the type of shallow thinking that stupid jokes like his betrayed, shallow thinking that normalized passing judgment on victims rather than focusing on what law enforcement should actually be concerned with—that is, conducting a full investigation and holding violent offenders responsible for their crimes.

But I didn't. I simply turned my back, picked up the last of my things, and walked away.

After all, what was the point? If I couldn't get an *agent* to understand the nuances of victim psychology in a case like this, then how could I ever hope to make a jury member—someone with much less training and experience—understand? How could I open someone's eyes to a truth they refused to see?

I'm not naïve. I know it's much easier to take the self-protective approach of narrowing one's vision so that the dark fringes of reality stay conveniently blurred. What's more, the Scott case was horrific. His brutal attacks and the psychological scars they left on his victims afterward—they all went far beyond the threshold of what most people were willing to think about or accept.

I understood this, yes—but looking away wasn't an option. I couldn't help resolve what I refused to acknowledge.

Truth and justice, I reminded myself.

Vincit omnia veritas.

Charlie Scott was the most textbook example of a confidence-style offender I'd seen up to that point. He was an Army private who used the authority of his position to coerce women into performing unwanted sexual acts. He was also a skillful escape artist—a modern-day Houdini who repeatedly vanished from jail cells time and time again.

In August 1992, for example, after being apprehended for felony theft and placed in the psychiatric wing of Fort Sill for examination, Scott managed to escape his cell, leaving only abandoned clothes in his place. He was quickly recaptured by United States marshals, and on September 17, 1992, the United States magistrate held a hearing that found Scott competent to conduct his initial appearance in federal court.

Days later, on September 23, 1992, he was transferred to United States military custody. Scott's federal indictment was dismissed, and he was charged as planned. However, he escaped yet again, this time managing to avoid recapture for more than two years, during which time he committed a series of increasingly horrific crimes that landed him a feature segment on an episode of *America's Most Wanted*.

Scott was born March 3, 1964, in Union Spring, Alabama. He was one of eight siblings—six sisters and two brothers—whose parents both worked outside the home for long hours, leaving the older children to help with chores and child care for the younger ones. Scott rebelled against this setup early on. He became involved in neighborhood gang activity while still a child, and fell deeper into gang life during his teens, right after his father died. Although he wasn't a particularly good student, Scott had a skill for deception. Right after high school, he even enlisted in the Army using his sister's name and Social Security number—Charlie Mae Scott—in order to conceal his criminal record.

As Charlie grew older, his deceptive and violent inclinations continued to escalate. He moved to Richmond, Virginia, changed his name, and spent his nights pretending to be a sex worker so he could get victims alone and rob them. He then moved to Alabama, where he impersonated an undercover officer and used coercion and lies to rape an underage girl—intimidating her into believing she'd be thrown into jail if she didn't have sex with him. Later on, in San Antonio, Texas, after being arrested on additional rape charges, Scott managed to escape confinement by faking seizures and then climbing out of the medical detention center through the overhead ductwork.

The list of horrific details goes on and on. But taking a more by-the-numbers approach, Scott, throughout his decade of active criminal activity, raped nearly a dozen women, mutilated his own fingers to avoid capture, and escaped from three jails. His elusive nature allowed him to tally up an encyclopedic list of charges: fraudulent enlistment, desertion (two specifications), armed robbery (three specifications), kidnapping (two specifications), burglary (two specifications), larceny, wrongful appropriation of an automobile, housebreaking, wrongful possession of a military identification card, wrongful and willful impersonation of a non-commissioned officer, indecent assault, escape from confinement (three specifications), and a charge for attempted escape from confinement.

It took the FBI's involvement to finally bring Scott into secure custody. And it was because of my connection with the Bureau that I was sought out as a testifying expert in December 1995, when he was to be held accountable for his crimes in a court of law.

Trial attorneys needed someone who could analyze and testify on the psychological aspects of his crimes, as well as the likelihood of his rehabilitation. They wanted me to provide expert testimony during a presentencing session—known as an Article 39a session in military cases—where I would speak to "rehabilitative potential of the accused." I'd be joined by BSU Supervisory Special Agent Alan Brantley, a former psychologist who evaluated offenders for the North Carolina Department of Corrections prior to joining the FBI. We decided that Brantley would dig into Scott's criminal background with the trial attorneys, and I'd interview the victims to prepare testimony based on their experiences.

It became clear right away that Scott took a deliberate approach to choosing his victims. He often targeted women who were active in the military, carefully taking the time to befriend them, earn their trust, and establish a sense of security before launching an attack.

One of Scott's earlier rapes became something of a blueprint for the many that would follow. The day before the attack, Scott approached two young women who were walking down the street in broad daylight. He said he was a police officer with a warrant and needed help finding a man named Huggy. He flattered the girls by telling them how cute they were, told them he'd pay them for their help, and then won them over by taking them to Hardees for something to eat.

Scott was smart, adaptable, and incredibly manipulative—a dangerous combination. He asked the girls to tell him about themselves, and when he learned that they were seventeen, he said that he was underage, too. He even made himself appear vulnerable by telling them what it was like in jail. Eventually, he asked one of the girls, Carylene, if she'd go on a date with him. She agreed, and when the two of them met up the next day, Scott initiated a role-playing game where he was the cop, she was the drug dealer, and the two of them rehearsed lines into a tape recorder. After a few minutes of this, Scott's true personality came out. He turned on Carylene, threatening her that he'd take the tape to the cops and have her arrested if she didn't have sex with him. She felt like she had no choice but to give in. She reported the rape a few days later.

This was far from the only time that Scott would resort to these cruel tactics to get what he wanted. Later that same year, he impersonated a drill sergeant and approached a lower-ranking army recruit named Pam. He pulled rank to force her to go on dates with him. Their get-togethers were casual at first, Pam said, but Scott quickly became aggressive and insisted that he wanted to be the father of Pam's children. Pam rebuffed him, saying that she wasn't ready to have sex with him yet. But Scott then over-powered her, forcibly removed her shorts and hid them, then informed her that he was going to bring her back to the barracks that way. After Scott raped her, he told her: "Don't be mad. It felt good for you, too." A few weeks later, he tried to rape her a second time, but she fought him off and managed to injure him. Scott apologized and said he was sorry for making her do something that she didn't want to do. Pam waited nearly a full month before reporting the sexual assaults to the Army.

Delayed reporting presented us with a big challenge in the Scott case. All but two of the victims were slow to contact author-ities, which is certainly understandable for those trying to process sexual trauma but does make it more difficult to prosecute the offenders. One was a third-party report, and another spoke with police only after her name was given in a statement by another victim.

Unfortunately, delayed reporting is fairly common in confidence-style assaults. It speaks to the preexisting trust between the victim and offender, and to the confusion that accompanies the violation of that trust. But despite being a normal psychological response, delayed reporting is widely misunderstood by both law enforce-ment and the greater public, and it's often used against the victim. The psychology behind this is simple: We don't want to deal with those types of horrifying realities, so we deny their very existence. We choose to protect ourselves and our sense of security, and in doing so, we leave victims even more vulnerable.

This rampant denial was especially prominent throughout the armed services during the time of Scott's case, when they still lacked transparency about the prevalence of sexual assault within their ranks. Military leaders would often conduct internal investigations in a manner that reinforced their own skepticism. They did this through the use of polygraphs—which was then standard practice when the victim and offender knew each other—but then they incorporated deliberately misleading techniques that skewed the end results. My interview with Robin, a later victim of Scott's, made this abundantly clear.

"What happened with the polygraph?" I asked her. "CID [U.S. Army Criminal Investigation Command] said you failed it."

Robin looked defeated. "A couple of things went wrong. I was tired and I was just agreeing with them. They would say, 'Maybe he didn't rape you.' And I said, 'Sure.' Or it was something along those lines. But then I signed the statement anyway."

"I see." I paused and looked down at my notes, giving her time to lead the conversation at her own pace.

"They kept coming up with reasons," Robin continued. "Like, ways to take it all back. They said I could have been feeling guilty or that I didn't put up enough of a fight or that I wasn't sure it was rape. I could tell they wanted me to agree with them."

"Did you agree?"

"I said it could be possible. They gave me two polygraphs. I was pretty confused on the whole issue."

"You signed a sworn statement that said you didn't know whether the first sergeant knew you objected to the sex."

"Because I knew I did poorly on the polygraphs and it made me doubt how I was feeling at the time and I was tired and so I signed it," Robin explained. "I should have been more in control. I was so intoxicated, and I do know better than to put myself in those situations. I was embarrassed and didn't want to go through all this. I've made mistakes in my life and I didn't want this to be another one."

————————

On the day of the presentencing session, the assistant trial counsel stated that I was "going to discuss the factors that lead to recidivism" by sex offenders and would testify that the appellant lacked rehabilitative potential. The military judge approved and noted that I had been qualified as an expert on the area of rape trauma.

Of course, I'd learned that you have to fight for every inch in legal battles. Nothing is given. Nothing is easy. So it was no surprise when the defense counsel pushed back by stating:

"We would definitely object to her testifying in that capacity [on rehabilitative potential]. She has not even so much as interviewed PFC Charlie Scott and cannot therefore testify about his rehabilitative potential. Your Honor, we would cite RCM 1001. It looks like it's—I think it's 1001(b)5(c), Your Honor."

The judge, however, citing *United States v. Stinson*, 34 MJ 233 (CMA 1992), dismissed the defense counsel's objection, stating that it wasn't necessary for an expert to conduct an interview to testify about a person.

Away from the jury, I told the judge about my studies concerning recidivism by sexual offenders and was then cross-examined extensively by the defense. After the judge ensured that I was not going to testify that appellant "should go to jail," the judge overruled the defense objection to my testimony as to recidivism and the potential for rehabilitation of sexual offenders. He noted that the defense's concern about my failure to interview the appellant personally would factor into the weight of this testimony.

Following this closed-door session, I then testified before the members of the court that I had never talked to the appellant, his family or friends, or even to the doctor who conducted the competency evaluation of the appellant. Though I reviewed statements made by the appellant, I never testified as to the content of any of those statements. My testimony went as follows:

Burgess: I have three brief documents from 1987 that—I have, I think it's a statement by him. It's an unsworn statement, and it's an evaluation done in November of 1987, and then from 1992, I have a psychiatrist's report of an examination that he did...and then I have the results of that from December 16th, 1992.

Prosecution: In your opinion, is the accused at a high risk or a low risk for re-offense?

Burgess: My opinion...

Defense: I object, Your Honor.

Military Judge: Overruled. Go on.

Burgess: My opinion is [that] he is at high risk for re-offense.

Prosecution: And why is that?

Burgess: That is based on the evidence on those three variables, that impulsivity. The evidence of that is his escape behavior in terms of four actually—one attempt and three completed. That's impulsivity. On anti-social behavior, the variables there are evidence of lying, evidence of manipulation, evidence of deception and I found evidence there of lying in terms of entrance into the military, also deception in terms of impersonating people that he was not, and manipulation, I found evidence of that in just reading one of the military records, and escalation of aggression. There was that in the offenses.

Prosecution: Is there an absolute cure for a sexual offender?

Burgess: There is no absolute cure, not only sex offenders but many other situations, but there is always the hope of rehabilitation to reduce the risk. What we try to do in any health situation is to reduce the risk of that behavior occurring again.

I concluded by stating that the appellant exhibited several of the various risk factors for re-offense, including his age—earlier intervention being better—and the fact that he'd committed multiple types of assault. Most police jurisdictions recognize several levels of assault charges including: simple assault, aggravated assault, assault with a deadly weapon, sexual assault, and felony assault. Depending on the fact of the case, a prosecutor then decides whether to charge the offense as a misdemeanor or a felony. The fact that the appellant had committed so many different kinds of assault, and to varying degrees, didn't necessarily inspire faith in the possibility of his rehabilitation.

On cross-examination, the defense tried to portray me as biased by noting that I was being paid by the prosecution for my analysis. This is a common tactic, and a flawed one. Many jurors assume that expert witnesses aren't paid for their work, and so when the defense brings it up in cross, it can make the jury doubt whether or not the witness has been incentivized to present information in a certain way.

Annoyed but calm, I responded to the defense like I always do, acknowledging that I received compensation for my expertise and time, not to sway the outcome of the case, and added that all expert witnesses are bound by strict ethical guidelines, guidelines which I took incredibly seriously.* I then explained that part of the basis for my opinion was the extensive catalogue of interviews I'd conducted with several of the accused's victims. I also acknowledged that the additional documents I examined were provided by the government, including a mental status evaluation in September 1987 and another one in 1992 completed by Dr. John Sparks. Here, the defense counsel's objection on the basis of hearsay was overruled by the judge. Neither the direct, cross, or redirect examination produced any evidence that I had access to privileged portions of a psychiatric examination of the appellant, which rendered my testimony admissible.

I rarely thought about the Scott case over the years. In truth, I preferred not to, given the especially violent nature of his crimes. But it occasionally came up for some reason or other. And whenever it did, it was invariably attached to the memory of that agent laughing and mocking Scott's victims as "typical women." This was particularly painful on October 12, 2023, when Scott pleaded guilty to charges of rape, kidnapping, and aggravated assault in

---

* This approach usually works, but not always. I remember one juror in particular who refused to listen to any expert because, as he yelled, "They're all paid and that means they're all compromised!" showing no self-awareness for the fact that *jurors are paid for their services as well.*

connection with an attack on a fifteen-year-old girl that occurred twenty-nine years prior.

The victim had been approached by Scott on her way home after helping her mother at work. He pointed a pistol at her, racked the gun, and threatened to kill her if she screamed. Once she was under his control, Scott forced the victim into the bushes and raped her. He then threatened that he would come back and kill her if she ever told anyone about the attack. It was only because a passing witness happened to see Scott coming out of the bushes and fixing his pants that the victim got immediate help from the authorities, which included the administration of a sexual assault kit.

Frustratingly, the case sat cold for sixteen years. Then, in March 2020, DNA from the sexual assault kit was tested against records of known sexual offenders, which identified Scott as a positive match. Additional DNA testing linked Scott to sexual assaults of several other victims during the same time period.

DNA testing is by no means a perfect tool. In fact, I've worked on many cases—quite a few of them with Kathleen Zellner, a wrongful-conviction lawyer based out of Chicago—where improper use of DNA evidence has led to years of wrongful imprisonment that shattered the lives of individuals, their families, and their communities. But used properly—as a tool, not as a catchall—DNA analysis can be transformative for both law enforcement and legal professionals.

What's important to understand, however, is that the characterization of DNA evidence shown in television and movies isn't true to the realities of the legal system in action. It's not as simple as that. As happened in the Scott case, it took nearly *two decades* for that DNA evidence to come to light. As our world becomes more automated, more digitized, and more artificial with each passing year, I hope we don't lose our humanity for gains we can't yet fully understand.

That's the paradox of progress. The better things get, the more we seem to despair.

CHAPTER 6

Duke University Lacrosse

When Jim Cooney's name flashed across my phone in the fall of 2006, my first thought was of convicted serial killer Henry Louis Wallace, aka "the Taco Bell Strangler," a prolific killer who took the lives of eleven women over a period of five years in the early 1990s.

Jim had been a member of Wallace's legal team alongside public defender Isabel Day, and together the two had been quick to realize how unique Wallace and his circumstances were. First, Wallace was Black, whereas most known serial killers at the time were white. And second, Wallace targeted victims who were close colleagues and friends—not just people he knew, but people who trusted him and whom Wallace, by all appearances, cared for deeply. Cooney was stumped by these variables. They deviated so far from the norm that he wasn't sure what to make of them. And so he reached out to me—along with my colleague, retired agent Robert Ressler—with the request that we do a formal evaluation of Wallace and give expert testimony about his behaviors, his victims, and whether he was sound of mind or suffered a condition of mental health.

Maybe Wallace is up for parole, I thought, glancing at the caller ID as I unhooked the receiver and cradled it between my shoulder and ear.

"Nope—no parole. And no updates on Wallace. He's not the reason I'm calling," Jim said, getting straight to the point. "I'm working on something new. It's a rape case involving students on the Duke University lacrosse team. I'm sure you're aware of it."

"Of course," I replied. "It's been all over the news."

That was no exaggeration. As soon as the story broke, the Duke case—in which several members of the lacrosse team were accused of rape—ignited a firestorm that played out in the media and all across the internet. Everyone from ABC to ESPN to *Newsweek* and the *New York Times* raced to publish strong opinions about, well, not the case exactly, but what the case signified on a cultural level in terms of racial tensions, sexual assault, and the privilege held by a select few. The Duke campus—polarized and galvanized—quickly became the epicenter of attention. Students began carrying WANTED posters showing the faces of the accused paired with signs that read CASTRATE. And before any evidence had even been brought to trial, presiding District Attorney Mike Nifong went out of his way to pour gasoline on the fire by granting dozens of interview requests with the media in which he expressed certainty that the players were guilty.

"Yeah, well, forget everything you've heard. There's not much evidence to support the media's version of events. I know it, and the prosecution knows it, too. The DA already let slip—and this was during a *nationally televised interview*, mind you—that he plans to defend his client's inconsistent allegations by saying it's a memory issue caused by rape and the accompanying trauma. But there's a big difference between memory issues and lying through your teeth.

"That's why I'm calling. I can't think of anyone better to rebut him than the person who introduced the concept of rape trauma syndrome into the scientific literature in the first place. I could really use your expertise on this one—both in terms of figuring out how to organize the evidence and at trial, to explain to the jury exactly why the accuser keeps changing her story. I need you to spell out what the accuser's behaviors mean so the jury can make an informed decision. If she's showing symptoms of rape trauma syndrome, that's one thing. But if there's something else going on, then that's the angle we'll pursue."

"I'm interested," I said. "Why don't you start at the beginning and tell me what you've got so far? We'll figure the rest out from there."

Jim, in his typically calm demeanor, laid out the basics of the case. His client, Reade Seligmann—a nineteen-year-old New Jersey native with wavy hair, a linebacker-sized build, and no prior arrests or criminal history—was one of three Duke lacrosse players accused of gang-raping an exotic dancer at a house party earlier that year. However, Seligmann categorically denied any wrongdoing. He claimed that he'd already left the party when the alleged rape supposedly occurred, and he said that he had cell phone data and receipts from an ATM that would prove his innocence. Notably, he and the other accused players had all cooperated with the police from the start of the case: allowing investigators to search their rooms, submitting to questioning, and offering to take a polygraph.

"The irony is that no one paid much attention to the allegations at first," Jim said. "Investigators and university officials both saw the charges as thin and unlikely to hold up to scrutiny. But a week later, the nature of the investigation began to shift."

Jim went on to describe how the accuser, on the night of the alleged attack, initially claimed she'd been raped, then changed her story to say that she'd been groped but that no one forced her to have sex, then *again* changed her story to say that she'd been raped. Two days later, in accordance with routine follow-up for claims of sexual assault, investigators met with the accuser in her home to hear her version of events. This time, sitting calmly, she was able to describe in greater detail how three men had attacked her in a bathroom and raped her orally, vaginally, and anally. She also remembered their names: Adam, Bret, and Matt. The investigators then showed her a photographic lineup of the Duke lacrosse players, but she wasn't able to identify any specific individuals as her attackers, saying that they all looked alike.

The case was still just a he-said-she-said at this point. So on March 23, ten days after the initial event, Durham assistant district attorney David Saacks took the definitive step of submitting a court order to request that the entire lacrosse team submit to DNA testing. The students were ordered to comply.

"One of the regional papers got word of the DNA testing and sent a photographer to get a shot of the forty-six players showing up at the crime lab. It was a bad look...like a parade of the guilty or something," Jim lamented. "And on March twenty-fifth, the same paper ran a follow-up that shifted public opinion even further. It profiled the accuser as a single mom doing whatever she could to provide for her family. The feeding frenzy started immediately after that. It's been one commentator after another competing to outdo each other in their condemnation of the defendants."

Jim was right about the media's spin on the story. I'd followed the coverage from the start and noticed the same shift in tone from routine campus complaint to nationwide reckoning on racial and class tensions. I think this stemmed from how the case had been initially represented to the public, which was that there *had* been a rape and that it *had* been committed by members of the Duke lacrosse team. The problem was that an allegation had been presented as fact. And this, in turn, split the Duke University campus and Durham community into sharply divided factions.

To make matters worse, the flames of tension were being stoked by Durham County district attorney Mike Nifong—up for reelection that year—and his overt habit of politicizing the case to fit his own personal agenda: insisting that the crimes against the dancer had occurred, that they were racially motivated, and that the accused lacrosse players were simply a group of privileged white men who'd taken advantage of a poor black woman.

"Don't get me wrong," Jim said. "It makes sense that charges were brought against these men. Especially when you factor in the hospital visit and the fact that the accuser had verified injuries consistent with rape. But for the DA to all but pronounce the men as guilty and for the media to just run with it—that's totally irresponsible. I mean, the case hasn't even gone to trial yet and we've already seen protests in front of one defendant's house, a mob confronting Seligmann at his court appearance, and even a few death threats. This one's as tense as I've ever seen it—there's a lot at stake here. I wouldn't blame you if you passed it up. Hell, *I* almost passed it up. But then I met with the Seligmann family and felt like I needed to see this one through. Reade's parents spoke about their son like he'd come down with a fatal disease. And Reade himself came across as sincere and completely upset. I just... there's more to this story than what's being reported."

"Come on, Jim. You know I've never paid much attention to the spectacle surrounding cases," I said. "Send over everything you've got. I'll give you my honest assessment as quickly as I can."

A week after that call, two large manila envelopes arrived at my office, each stuffed full of case records, witness interviews, photographs, and official investigative reports. There was also a handwritten note explaining that the case's three lead lawyers—Jim Cooney, Wade Smith, and Brad Bannon—were dividing their defense into layers of expertise that would best match the DA's anticipated approach.

My job, as the note made clear, was twofold. First, I needed to put together an analysis of the accuser's psychiatric history based on police reports, medical files, and other publicly available records. Second, I needed to create a report that categorically accounted for each and every physical and psychological effect the accuser had shown during the wake of the alleged attack. This was where my clinical expertise came into play. I was one of the country's most prominent experts on rape trauma syndrome. Like Jim said, I'd spent years assessing and treating victims of abuse, and from this I'd devised an entire lexicon of language to understand the specific nature of rape trauma syndrome in all its varied forms.

In other words, I knew what I was talking about. I'd be ready for trial. If the prosecution intended to build their case around the idea of rape trauma syndrome, they'd better be damn sure to know what they were talking about as well.

March 13, 2006, was a warm day in Durham, North Carolina. It was spring break, the Duke University campus was mostly empty, and the men's lacrosse team had just finished practice when they decided to get together at the team captain's house for a cookout and party. After several hours of drinking, one of the players used an alias to call a local escort service and arranged for two exotic dancers to show up for entertainment. Shortly after 11:00 p.m., Kim Pittman—a thirty-one-year-old dancer who went by the stage name "Nikki"—arrived at the team captain's house. Half an hour and three additional calls to the escort service later, Nikki's partner, twenty-seven-year-old Crystal Mangum, was dropped off at the lacrosse house. Both women were given $400 in cash, then shown to a bathroom where they could change their clothes.

It was just before midnight when Nikki and Crystal entered the living room. They'd been hired to dance and to strip, but Crystal was unsteady on her feet and fell to the floor. Immediately, several lacrosse players laughed and began shouting lewd comments. Nikki and Crystal ignored this at first. But the shouts and catcalling intensified until one of the attendees held up a broomstick and told the women they should use it as a sex toy. Nikki got upset at this comment and put an end to the performance early, taking Crystal with her to the back of the house to collect their belongings.

What happened between midnight and about 1:00 a.m. is less clear. Fragments of information—official phone records, time-verified photos and videos, and other electronic bits of trace evidence collected from various individuals at the party—begin again at 12:26 a.m., when Crystal placed a call to the escort service. At 12:30 a.m., a series of photos show Crystal standing outside the lacrosse house on the back porch. Then, at 12:31 a.m., there's a short video of Crystal telling someone "I'm a cop," followed by slurred speech as she sways and struggles to keep her balance. Witness interviews corroborate that at 12:42 a.m., several party attendees helped Crystal walk to Nikki's car and placed her in the front seat. There was shouting back and forth. And finally, at 12:53 a.m., phone records show that Nikki called 911 to report a group of white men yelling racial comments from outside the lacrosse house on North Buchanan Boulevard.

Digital trace evidence during this same timeframe shows glimpses of Reade Seligmann's whereabouts, too. At 12:05 a.m., phone records reveal that Seligmann initiated a series of calls to his girlfriend on his phone. At 12:14 a.m., Seligmann called a taxi to pick him up, along with another party attendee. At 12:24 a.m., bank records show Seligmann making a withdrawal from an ATM. According to the taxi driver, Seligmann then got back into the taxi and made another stop at a restaurant to pick up food, then got back in the same vehicle and was dropped off at his dormitory at 12:46 a.m.

The data paints a similar picture of David Evans and Collin Finnerty, the other two lacrosse players accused of raping Crystal Mangum. For Evans, phone records show him spending sixteen minutes talking to his girlfriend on the phone starting at 12:34 a.m. And for Finnerty, records indicate that he made several calls and then left the party by 12:27 a.m., at which point he met up with another group of lacrosse players to get food from a nearby restaurant.

I put down the reports to make a quick note. Certainly it was possible that Crystal had been sexually assaulted at the party. But comparing the evidential data to Crystal's own allegation that Evans, Finnerty, and Seligmann had all held her in the bathroom and raped her orally, vaginally, and anally that night—the timing didn't add up. Still, the psychology of traumatic experiences is a complicated thing. Memories of trauma tend toward fluidity and self-protection rather than clarity or what's commonly described as "fixed." They're amoeba-like in a way, often obscuring pain and the overwhelming reality of trauma, never taking on a fully realized shape.

Knowing all that, I wasn't ruling out the possibility of assault. But if it happened, it happened different than in Crystal's memory.

The fragmented hour of the lacrosse party gave way to a cohesive narrative at 1:22 a.m. on March 14. That was when the Durham Police Department received a 911 call from a supermarket security guard about an unconscious woman in someone's car, parked about a mile from the Duke campus.

Sgt. John Shelton was first to the scene. According to his

report, Shelton was directed to a dark-colored Honda owned by Kim "Nikki" Pittman. Upon questioning the vehicle's driver, he was given a vague explanation that they'd offered the passenger a ride home because she was so inebriated. Shelton then went around to the passenger side and found Crystal Mangum slumped over in her seat, wearing a red negligee, no undergarments, and a single high-heeled shoe.

"She's breathing and appears to be fine," he radioed back to the dispatcher. "She's not in distress. She's just passed-out drunk."

But the more Shelton observed Mangum, the more he began to suspect that she was faking unconsciousness to avoid a confrontation. He'd seen plenty of passed-out drunks before. Mangum, however, looked tense rather than relaxed. And the pattern of her breathing wasn't steady. Shelton decided to put an ammonia capsule under Mangum's nose to see how she'd respond. As he'd expected, Mangum suddenly began to breathe through her mouth—a typical response when someone's faking unconsciousness. Then she started acting aggressive.

"I grabbed the female and attempted to pull her from the vehicle," Shelton wrote in his report. "She grabbed the emergency brake with her left hand and would not come out of the car. At this point, I applied a bent-wrist come-along to her right hand and arm. As I applied pressure, she became responsive, and eventually I was able to get her out of the car. Once she was out of the car, I released the pressure and she collapsed to the ground."

By then, two other officers had arrived on the scene. They agreed that the best course of action was to check Mangum into the Durham Center Access facility, a nearby substance-abuse and psychological crisis center that was well equipped to handle this type of situation. They drove the short distance, and during the standard check-in process, a staff nurse asked a nonstandard question—the type of leading question that can bias a patient's response and create a whole tangle of on-the-record inaccuracies.

"During the check-in process, the victim was asked if something had happened to her and she said, 'Yes,' " the attending officer noted in his report. "[The nurse] then asked if she had been raped, and she stated, 'Yes.' "

At 2:31 that morning, Mangum was taken to the emergency room at Duke University Medical Center. Sgt. John Shelton was right beside her in the ER. Shelton assessed that Mangum was now coherent enough to respond to investigative questioning. He asked about her allegations of rape. Mangum recanted, saying that she'd been hired to "put on a show" and that "some of the guys" had "groped her" and had taken her money, but that she hadn't been raped. After a few additional questions, Shelton then called the police station to report that Mangum was recanting her statement of being raped. However, while Shelton was out of the room, Mangum reversed her story again, telling a doctor that she *had* been raped, and adding that she would no longer respond to questions from Durham Police.

This shifting narrative continued to go back and forth for the next eight hours. At one point, Mangum told a Duke University police officer that she'd been raped by twenty men at the lacrosse house that evening. Then the number went down to five. Then three. She also told doctors about the "severe pain" she was feeling because of the assault. However, her examiners noted that she "did not exhibit any of the symptoms normally associated with severe pain" and that her "behavior was highly atypical for a rape victim who lacked any bruising, bleeding, tearing or other visible physical injury."

Mangum was discharged from the hospital shortly thereafter. And at around 3:00 a.m., Durham Police and Duke University Police engaged in an extensive briefing of the case, agreeing that there was no evidence to proceed with a rape investigation and that charges were unlikely to exceed misdemeanor simple assault against the occupants of the lacrosse house at 610 North Buchanan.

———————

It's not uncommon for victims to experience confusion after a sexual assault, so that part didn't particularly stand out to me. After all, this is a fairly common feature of rape trauma syndrome: confusion and difficulty remembering every detail of what happened during an attack. What surprised me, though, was how wildly variable the allegations were from one interview to the next. Victims of sexual assault tend to be consistent in what they remember and what they don't. But Mangum's story was far outside the norm. It was unlike anything I'd learned about victims of sexual assault over decades of research and experience. Again, this didn't necessarily mean Mangum was being disingenuous or making things up. But it *did* challenge prevailing truths. And that made me wonder if Occam's razor was coming into play.

Sticking to the task at hand, I proceeded to do a deep dive into Mangum's mental health history, which I knew could provide some helpful background context going back to her teenage years. On August 18, 1996, eighteen-year-old Mangum went to the police to file a report on her ex-boyfriend. She claimed that three years earlier, when she was just fourteen, her ex—who was seven years older than her—had raped her with two of his friends while she was helping them sell drugs. Mangum went on to explain that she was coming to the police now, after all this time, because she wanted to hold the men accountable so she could move on with her life. However, she didn't follow through on pressing charges. As she later told the Durham investigators, she'd dropped the case after the police explained that the men involved were already imprisoned for other crimes, and the time lapse would make it difficult, if not impossible, for her to prove anything.

In the wake of that initial allegation of sexual assault against her boyfriend, Mangum's father described noticing a stark change in his daughter. She'd become suicidal, and she began seeing a psychiatrist who diagnosed her with bipolar disorder and pre-scribed her medication to manage the trauma from the attack.

Maybe that's it, I thought, putting down the report to allow the larger picture to come into focus. Maybe what Mangum was really experiencing was a delayed onset of trauma caused by a flashback to the gang rape she'd experienced as a teenager. It made sense given her history with her boyfriend and clinical records of mental health issues. And it also made sense given that victims of sexual assault don't always experience their response to trauma all at once. In fact, in some cases, a delayed onset of rape trauma syndrome or PTSD can start years after the initial event. That would explain Mangum's inconsistent story and her inability to remember specific details about the alleged assault.

I'd seen this before, too. Mangum displayed all the signs of a neuropsychiatric disorder known as confabulation—unintentionally creating false memories by layering one memory over gaps in another. Mangum wasn't fabricating an accusation. She was simply blurring her memories of being raped as a teenager with a false memory of what happened at the lacrosse house that night.

That was my working theory, anyway. So I went back to the reports to see what else I could find.

Despite being assaulted as a teenager and dealing with lasting ramifications from the attack, Mangum went on to graduate from high school, got married, joined the Navy, and began two years of active duty in the summer of 1997. She was trained to operate radios in Virginia; later on, she was stationed on an ammunition ship off the coast of California. Unfortunately, her frequent tours at sea took a toll on her marriage, and on June 16, 1998, tensions reached a breaking point when Mangum accused her husband of threatening to kill her and pressed charges. Her case was dropped after she failed to appear at the hearing, and the two separated after just seventeen months of marriage. Shortly after that, Mangum became pregnant with the child of a fellow sailor and was discharged from the Navy.

Mangum returned home and supported herself and her child by working at a topless dance club. She had several run-ins with the law, including one time where she stole a cab and led the police on a wild chase. She was arrested, and while she was in custody, she was found to have a blood-alcohol level well over the legal limit. During questioning, she passed out and was taken to a hospital to recover. The manager of the strip club reported that this kind of behavior wasn't unusual, as she frequently drank to excess and passed out during her performances.

But it wasn't quite as simple as this, of course. In 2005, the year before the Duke incident, Mangum was hospitalized with what her mother described as a nervous breakdown, and was subsequently diagnosed with bipolar disorder. Her relatives argued that this picture of her being an out-of-control, unstable woman was completely untrue, describing her instead as a hard-working single mother who was genuinely trying to support her family and improve herself. In 2004, she'd earned an associate degree from Durham Technical Community College. Now she was in her second year as a full-time student at North Carolina Central University, studying police psychology and maintaining a 3.0 grade point average.

In addition to her mental well-being, I knew it was also important to consider her physical well-being—that is, her level of intoxication at the time of the incident. Mangum's fellow dancer, Nikki, told police that Crystal was "clearly sober" when she arrived at the lacrosse house—a description confirmed by a next-door neighbor—but became glassy-eyed, "talking crazy," and was "basically out of it" within the hour. Another witness report from a partygoer added that she appeared impaired, eventually passing out on a porch at the lacrosse house. A security guard confirmed these assessments, saying Mangum appeared "out of it" when she was driven to the parking lot of a nearby grocery store to sober up.

When Mangum was admitted to the hospital, she originally told ER doctors that she was "drunk and did not feel pain." In follow-up interviews, though, she informed police that she'd had only one or two beers before the party, along with Flexeril—a prescription drug known to enhance the effects of alcohol—plus a mixed drink when she arrived. The excessive level of intoxication as reported by police, witnesses, and hospital staff, however, just didn't align with Mangum's statement. And in fact, drug testing revealed that upon her admittance to the hospital, she'd ingested a dangerous mixture of substances, including Ambien, methadone, Paxil, amitriptyline, and antipsychotic medications such as Seroquel. Was Mangum intentionally leaving out the extent of this debilitating cocktail, or did she genuinely not remember? Or was she potentially drugged?

There was one other significant detail that stood out to me from the case reports: Mangum had never volunteered that she was raped. The records showed that she was asked if she was raped by police and hospital staff, and that she answered yes. Effectively, this meant that the original accusation wasn't actually hers.

As an expert in the field of sexual violence, I know the ways victims respond to trauma can be complicated and even seem contradictory at times. Sometimes, the victim's mind closes in on itself, becoming self-protective, distancing itself from the horrible experiences an individual is forced to endure. But through my years of study, I'd come to understand that this was a logical psychological process.

And that's what had bothered me most about the Duke case from the outset. There was trauma, yes. But the way Mangum expressed this trauma lacked the familiar patterns and behaviors of rape victimology that experience had taught me to expect. The only way it made sense was that Mangum was truly experiencing a delayed onset of rape trauma syndrome caused by flashbacks to being assaulted by her boyfriend when she was fourteen.

Add to that the layer of bias that had been injected into the case. That was a real concern, too. The intake nurse should never have asked Mangum if she'd been raped. Lead-in questions like that are a major factor in cases of false allegation. They have a way of setting the trajectory of a case in motion before investigators can even get a lay of the land. And once that happens—once sides have been taken and reputations are on the line—it can be next to impossible to get a case back on track.

My goal, to be clear, wasn't to discredit Mangum or villain-ize her in any way. My goal was simply to uncover the truth. The truth showed that Mangum had lived a rough life and persevered in the face of more challenges than seemed fair. But truth also needs to remain objective, and the objective truth of the events that transpired on the night of March 13 stood in stark contrast to Mangum's allegations of rape.

So if Mangum hadn't been assaulted, then why did she go along with the accusation? I could think of a few reasons. She might have simply said yes to the initial question because of how intoxicated she was at the time. Then it's possible that she didn't fully remember what happened after she sobered up and just got swept away in the momentum of the story. Another thing that could explain her compliance might be her history of mental health struggles. Perhaps she didn't really understand the question or was afraid to answer in the negative. It was also conceivable that she was responding positively to the question because she'd had a prior sexually victimizing situation. Lastly, I couldn't com-pletely dismiss the possibility that she might've simply wanted to get out of this situation and agreed to the question as the path of least resistance. People do that—*all the time*. Especially when they feel shame or guilt and simply want to avoid confronting those feelings in any meaningful way. But the theory I was still leaning most heavily toward was delayed onset of rape trauma syndrome. It checked all the boxes. And it seemed like the only way all the pieces of the puzzle fit together.

———————

I wanted to test out my early impressions of the case, so I decided to reach out to a former colleague, Roy Hazelwood, as a sounding board. Hazelwood and I had worked together on standardizing the methodology of rape investigations during our time at the BSU. Basically, this meant that we'd created strategies and procedures for how law enforcement should best investigate these types of cases while also taking a trauma-informed approach to the victims involved. I trusted Hazelwood. He was a straight shooter and a good friend. Plus, whereas I was spending most of my time nowadays testifying as an expert in courtroom trials, Hazelwood was still lecturing and working closely with the FBI, which meant that he could offer a uniquely investigative perspective.

"Roy. It's Ann. I'm working on the Duke lacrosse case. Do you have a minute?"

"Of course you are," Hazelwood said. "Are you with the prosecution or the defense?"

"Defense. They called me first. And after reading the case files and SANE report, I think it's probably the right side to be on. The accusations are sending up a lot of red flags."

SANE reports, in which a specially trained Sexual Assault Nurse Examiner examines a suspected victim of rape and collects forensic evidence, had only become common in hospitals starting in the early 1990s. But the practical applications of these reports quickly made them a standard of victim care. They were an official record containing evidence collection, medical findings, victim injuries, and the designated treatment plan—all perfectly preserved for whatever investigative or legal proceedings might follow.

"The SANE exam was done on the night Crystal Mangum arrived at Duke University Medical Center," I explained to Hazelwood, getting him up to speed. "It was administered by Tara Levicy, a SANE in training, and observed by resident Dr. Julie Manly. The pelvic examination revealed diffuse edema in the vaginal walls. There was no anal trauma. Levicy took photographs to document the examination, but they only show a few nonbleeding scratches and bruises on Mangum's knee and heel."

"How does the lack of forensic findings match up to the accuser's report of the attack?" Hazelwood asked me.

"Not very consistently," I responded. "Mangum's details keep shifting. She started off with a vague description of how the rape occurred with three men in a small bathroom, and said that she hit her head on a sink. But the SANE doesn't note any head or facial bruises."

"Okay. So the SANE doesn't corroborate an injury to her head," he began. "Maybe that's just her memory being distorted by trauma."

"Maybe. But Levicy's report lists several additional claims that weren't corroborated by physical evidence, either. For example, Mangum claimed that she last had intercourse a week before the attack, that there was no digital penetration or penetration by a foreign object, that her assailants hadn't used condoms, that at least one of the assailants had ejaculated, that one of the assailants said he was getting married the following day, and that she'd experienced vaginal, oral, and anal penetration."

"No physical evidence backing up any of these claims?"

"Nothing substantive," I replied. "The SANE doesn't indicate sexual assault."

"Hold on a second." He stopped me. "How much of what you're telling me is from the SANE versus interviews or other reports?"

"That's part of what makes this case so unusual," I admitted. "Since Levicy was a SANE in training, her report isn't solely her own. Some of it involved other medical staff who weren't familiar with SANE protocol, but stepped in anyway because of Levicy's inexperience. And some of it involved investigators. That lack of continuity and trust could definitely play a role in why the accuser's story keeps growing and changing throughout the report. It almost seems like these investigators and medical staff helped fill in the key details of her story, even if they didn't intend to."

Hazelwood and I had worked together for so long, I could all but *hear* him nodding his head at this point as he took in all the information. "So," he said at last, "clearly, Mangum was asked a lot of investigative-style questions rather than open-ended ones to tell her story herself—or at least that's how it sounds to me, given the nature of the details in the report. Is that your sense, too?"

"Yes. That's the overall pattern I'm seeing with this case," I replied. "Whatever happened that night, we never got a chance to hear it in Mangum's own words—not really, anyway. There was always something getting in the way, whether it was her intoxication, or the heavy-handed involvement of investigators and other medical professionals throughout the SANE. Then down the line, there's also the media's one-sided involvement, and then the

Durham County district attorney, Nifong, politicizing the case for his own agenda. That's a lot of pressure on our victim here. She was becoming a symbol for larger cultural conversations about rape and privilege. Combine all that with the mix of psychiatric variables I described, and it only makes sense that she'd stick to the prevailing narrative. Especially if she couldn't really remember what happened herself."

"I see where you're going with this," Hazelwood agreed. "Media pressure, prior accusations of assault, a history of mental health. If she's struggling with an unresolved trauma, that could be where this lacrosse story is coming from. She's layering one memory over the other."

"Thanks, Roy," I said, relieved. "Good to know we're on the same page."

Because I'd already aligned myself with the defense, I knew I wouldn't be able to conduct my own interview of Mangum for the case—prosecutors rarely allow defense experts such access to their clients. But I still had plenty of material to work with. The files Jim sent me were more than enough to build out my testimony. They formed a narrative of Mangum's mental health and trauma over the years that led to a rational conclusion of false allegations levied against the lacrosse players. Psychiatrically, my findings were sound. And as for the investigation, my findings were well supported by trace evidence, witness testimony, and a whole slew of police reports that mapped out not only a timeline of events but also a profile of Mangum herself. What was less clear, however, was what supporting evidence the prosecution felt they had that could help them win the case. What was I missing?

At this point in my prep, I decided to take a closer look into the key legal players involved in the case. That type of due diligence is important. It helps account for the human element of a trial, that variable of *how* evidence is presented, not just *what* evidence is presented. I always felt that if I could understand the people involved—their track records, their motivations—I could use that information to develop case-specific strategies and to be better prepared when I took the stand as an expert witness. Sometimes it was as simple as anticipating the opposition's strategy. Other times, it helped steel me against malicious attacks on my credibility. And on occasion, it revealed whole other layers entirely, like it did with Durham County district attorney Mike Nifong.

The fact that Nifong was presiding over this case during an election year was a red flag on its own. Of course, political entanglement is fairly common with trials. But what's far less common is a DA taking every opportunity to meet with the media and declare unequivocally that a crime has occurred. The politics motivating Nifong's involvement were obvious. He all but said it himself in one of many interviews, pronouncing: "The reason I decided to take it over myself was the combination gang-like rape activity accompanied by the racial slurs and general racial hostility." He then took his own moral self-righteousness a step further, noting that he was "disappointed that no one has been enough of a man to come forward."

Nifong also used the media as a tool to systematically get ahead of case evidence by presenting it with a narrative spin. One particular example that stood out to me was during a nationally televised news appearance on March 29. In response to host Dan Abrams's question about whether or not he believed a rape had occurred, Nifong responded, "I am convinced that there was a rape, yes, sir... The circumstances of the case are not suggestive of the alternate explanation that has been suggested by some of the members of the situation. There is evidence of trauma in the victim's vaginal area that was noted when she was examined by a nurse at the hospital. And her general demeanor was suggestive of the fact that she had been through a traumatic situation."

If you only listened to this interview, it would make sense to naturally take the prosecution's side. But there were a number of key points that Nifong failed to mention, like the fact that he still hadn't taken time to speak with Mangum directly. He also conveniently neglected to add that she'd made a number of inconsistent statements about the event, that no DNA evidence recovered during her SANE matched any of the lacrosse players, that the second exotic dancer who was with her dismissed Mangum's allegations of rape as "a crock," or that Mangum had experienced significant difficulties in identifying her accused aggressors, even though she was given the opportunity to do so across several police lineups.

Cooney saw right through Nifong's approach from the start. It didn't seem to matter whether or not all the evidence supported the accuser's account, the prosecution had decided the lacrosse players were guilty and was dead set on proving it in a court of law. Even so, Cooney also realized that the challenge here was about more than just the incident itself, since this case represented a "perfect storm" of race, class, and gender issues that "appealed to our worst thoughts about male athletes and underprivileged women of color."

"It's a case where everyone's already chosen sides," he explained during our next call. "That doesn't give us much room to work with."

"Come on, Jim. Nifong can play to people's ideologies all he wants—it won't hold much weight in a courtroom if he can't use evidence to support it. Yes, there's a lot of sympathy for Mangum. But we're not dismissing the idea of rape. And we're certainly not getting into a 'battle of the experts' with whoever the prosecution decides to bring in. We're simply following the facts to their logical conclusion. Delayed-onset trauma syndrome caused by a flashback to the gang rape she experienced when she was fourteen. That's the only explanation that makes sense. I've already narrowed my focus to the accuser's psychiatric history, her post-incident response, and her SANE exam. That gives us *plenty* to work with. It avoids a 'battle of the experts' where we get bogged down by the nuances of rape trauma syndrome.

"And besides," I added, "Mangum's postincident response, her SANE report, and the blatant inconsistences of her story—none of it supports her allegations. It's all just contradictions. I can explain that to a jury. And I'm confident you'll be able to show the holes in the defense's story if you put together a timeline of the night's events compared to the official record of what Mangum actually said."

"Makes sense," Cooney agreed. "But aren't you at all concerned that the jury will already have their minds made up before the trial even begins?"

"It's fine if they do," I said. "In fact, it's probably even better in that the weight of expectation all lies with the prosecution. But here's the thing, Jim: Strategies that work in the media rarely work in the courtroom. There's burden of proof, hard evidence, and a reality that exists beyond the simplicities of media slant. The prosecution's got nothing more than a house of cards. It's a false story just waiting to collapse."

While I was building out my testimony, Cooney combed through stacks of physical and digital evidence to piece together a verifiable chain of events that occurred on March 13, 2006. He'd been given access to three digital cameras that police had seized from the house after the party, and one of these contained time-stamped photos that corroborated that the women performed only until 12:04 a.m. Then, according to a cell phone bill, between 12:05 and 12:13, Cooney's client, Seligmann, made eight brief calls, each of thirty-six seconds or less—six of them to his girlfriend's number, and one to a taxi at 12:14 a.m. He left the party shortly afterward, which was confirmed by the taxi driver himself. Cooney had also secured an ATM photo showing Seligmann withdrawing cash during the time of the alleged rape. To further bolster his timeline, he uncovered call logs from the accuser to her escort service voice mail in which she checked to see if she had more jobs lined up for the night, as well as calls made to her father during the time she claimed she was being raped.

The electronic "tracks" left by the four involved parties—the alleged victim and the three accused—cast serious doubt on the prosecution's timeline. All in all, Cooney and his colleagues were able to isolate only a two-minute span when all three accused players were in the same room at the same time, let alone in the same room as the accuser—a far cry from the thirty minutes she'd initially claimed.

The digital record contradicted more than just Mangum's timeline of events, it also contradicted her statements about the nature of the attack itself. Mangum claimed that her rapists had hit, kicked, and strangled her, before assaulting her anally, vaginally, and orally. But the recovered time-stamp photos showed clear evidence of cuts and bruises on Mangum's legs from the moment she first arrived at the house. A series of photos taken after the alleged incident further complicated her account: At 12:31 a.m., she was pictured smiling and calm, wearing skimpy clothes but not looking disheveled or out of order; at 12:37 a.m., she was now lying on her side on the back stoop after an apparent fall, with new cuts and scrapes; and then at 12:41, one of the lacrosse players was helping Mangum into a car.

The case was quickly imploding. All forty-six white Duke lacrosse players submitted to DNA testing, and yet no foreign DNA "was found on or inside the accuser or on her clothing" in the first place—a fact that prosecutors initially hid from the defense. What's more, the accuser's ever-evolving accounts made the claim that she was raped at the Duke lacrosse party even more doubtful. Had she been assaulted by three players, or five, as she later said? Did anyone force her to have sex?

Months after the indictment of the three lacrosse players, the accuser wavered in her story once again, saying she was unsure whether she was penetrated at all. Although the players still faced kidnapping and sexual assault charges, the accuser's revelation forced Nifong to drop the rape charges completely.

The case fell apart so quickly that I never got a chance to deliver the testimony I'd prepared. Not that I was surprised by the development—there were so many holes in the investigation to begin with that the outcome was inevitable once good legal counsel got involved. But despite never playing a role publicly in the case, my behind-the-scenes involvement let me see firsthand how detrimental false allegations could be. A grand jury had indicted three young men. Their community had turned on them. The media had all but convicted them. And their lives would never be the same—regardless of the legal outcome.

I understood the high stakes at play here. It was why I'd agreed to take a look at the case in the first place. But I also understood the importance of approaching every single case with an open mind. The estimates of false rape allegations range between 2 and 8 percent. That means that there's a 2 to 8 percent chance that the accused party is actually the victim, that the script's been flipped. My goal has always been to fight for the truth—and stand up for the victim. In order to do that, it's essential to ensure that the facts come first, even and *especially* if the facts conflict with the prevailing narrative.

Mangum was never charged for reporting false rape allegations, but the guilty associations that lingered on members of the Duke lacrosse team exemplified a harsh reality: Once an allegation exists, it can quickly take on a life of its own. This was essentially a worst-case scenario in which three systems of control—the university, the media, and the criminal justice system—failed to maintain the basic protections of *all* the individuals involved in a case.

On April 11, 2007, North Carolina attorney general Roy Cooper dropped all charges against the three former Duke University lacrosse players. Standing in front of a swarm of press, Cooper announced: "We believe these three individuals are innocent of these charges." He then added that "the inconsistencies were so significant and so contrary to the evidence that we have no credible evidence that an attack occurred in that house on that night."

I was watching the televised conference when Cooney called to see if I'd heard the news, and to add that Nifong was being stripped of his law license and going to jail for a day for criminal contempt for lying about the DNA evidence.

"I keep reflecting back to where we were a year ago, when we were begging Nifong to look at the truth and look at the facts," Cooney said. "But he wasn't interested. He covered his ears with his hands. He was committed to doing exactly what he pleased."

But Nifong wasn't the only one to blame here. Neither was Mangum. In order for things to spiral to this magnitude, a *lot* of people had to drop the ball. The university failed to protect its students from a mob demanding quick justice. The media reflexively bought the narrative of pampered white student athletes run amok. The criminal justice system failed to accord defendants the basic protections offered by North Carolina rules of criminal procedure. Each of these failures, as we learned, compounded the others.

That's a difficult reality to accept—that our justice system isn't perfect, that sometimes innocent people slip through the cracks. I think about this often when I'm taking on a case for the defense.

Because I get it. I understand the confusion: "Why aren't you defending the victim? Who cares about the offender? Why waste your efforts on them?" And I guess that speaks to the power of media in certain cases. Sometimes it's easier to get caught up in the narrative rather than the facts themselves.

But that's why it's so important to keep an open mind. You never know who the victim might end up being. Sometimes the most stunning realizations are the ones hiding in plain sight.

CHAPTER 7

The Dismantling of "America's Dad"

You look stressed," Bill Cosby said, flashing a made-for-TV smile as he held out three blue pills in the palm of his hand. "Here. These will help you relax."

"Are they herbal?"

"Yeah," Cosby said. "Just swallow them. They're your friends."

"I, umm..."

Andrea Constand had no idea what to expect when Cosby invited her to his home to discuss a potential career in sports broadcasting. But it wasn't this. It wasn't wine and pills and the two of them alone in his dimly lit suburban Philadelphia mansion on a cold January night in 2004.

"Here," Cosby insisted, his face still rigid with a smile as he glanced back and forth between her and the pills.

Constand hesitated. She was a thirty-one-year-old athlete who had always taken meticulous care of her body. She didn't take pills—never had—but she was standing in the presence of one of the most iconic celebrities in the world and felt like she didn't have much of a choice. So she swallowed them like she'd been told.

A moment passed.

"How do you feel?" Cosby asked.

She tried to speak, but her words spilled out in a thick slur, her mouth feeling fuzzier and fuzzier with every breath.

"Let me help." Cosby guided her to the couch and told her to lay down.

She could barely walk. Her arms felt numb. She couldn't think.

Then the world went dark.

Constand woke up several hours later in the silence of pre-dawn dark. She was on the same couch, but her top had been pulled over her breasts and her bra was unclasped. She felt completely disheveled. Nothing about the situation made any sense. How had she ended up there?

Suddenly, a brutal memory seared its way to the front of her mind: She remembered being jolted awake by Cosby putting his arms around her, sliding his hand down into her pants, and sticking his fingers into her vagina. Blinking in disbelief, she received another flash, this time of Cosby taking her hand in his and positioning it around his penis, using it to masturbate.

She was horrified.

More memories flickered in and out, flashing across her consciousness like old, staticky film reels projected on screen. She felt nauseous. She closed her eyes as tightly as she could to block out the world and everything racing through her head. But when she opened them again, she found herself back on the couch, more disheveled than she'd felt just moments before.

Home, she thought. *I need to get home.*

———

Like the rest of the world, I was shocked when I first heard the allegations of sexual assault against Bill Cosby. It wasn't that my idea of him was crafted solely from his wholesome on-screen reputation, either. Rosalyn Watts, a close friend of mine and fellow faculty during my years at the University of Pennsylvania, had dated Cosby in high school and sometimes shared stories about what he was like back then versus the public image he'd cultivated, thanks to his iconic role on *The Cosby Show*.

They'd met while Rosalyn—Roz, as I knew her—was attending an all-girls Catholic high school in Philadelphia, which happened to be affiliated with the all-boys Catholic high school Cosby attended. Roz described the Cosby she knew as kind, charming, and a little bit goofy. He could be shy, too—she once described how Cosby became flushed and nervous when he'd invited her to his high school prom—but he wasn't the type to get angry or aggressive. From what Roz said, everything about their relationship seemed pretty typical for kids that age. They hung out with friends, went to movies, and spent long hours talking on the phone. They even managed to end things on good terms, with Roz breaking off the relationship when they both went off to separate colleges. Shortly after, Cosby went on to date Camille Olivia Hanks, the woman who would become his wife.

Roz was the first person I called after hearing about the case in January 2005. I had no professional involvement at the time. Mostly, I just wanted to see how my friend was handling the news and to hear her thoughts about the accusations. I knew she'd give me her honest opinion, and she did.

"I'm not sure what to make of it," she admitted, still shell-shocked. "He was always such a gentleman to me. You know this—how we stayed in touch, and how he called from time to time to check in on how things were going in my career. But he was never inappropriate. And he certainly never tried to drug me or anything. Honestly, he *was* the Cliff Huxtable character he played on TV. That's just who he was!"

At the end of our call, Roz and I both agreed that all we could do about the accusations was keep an open mind. We rarely talked about it after that. Roz had said her piece, and everything else was speculation. And so I didn't think much about the Cosby case in the years that followed.

That is, until June 2016.

That was when a call from Andrea Constand's lawyers lit up my phone screen. They needed a consulting expert, someone who could talk to Constand and give a professional assessment of her overall mental health. Was I interested?

"Of course," I said. "But why reopen the case now?"

Apparently a lot had happened both publicly and behind the scenes since Constand was attacked back in 2004. Dozens of other women had come forward to accuse Cosby of sexual assault, culminating in something more than just Cosby's precipitous fall from grace—something like a widespread cultural shift in which victims were starting to receive support rather than belittle-ment for standing up against their assailants. Couple this with a newfound media interest in the case after more than a decade of deafening silence, and the timing finally felt right for Constand to share her truth with the world.

"Are you sure your client's ready to share her story?" I asked.

"That's what we'd like you to tell us," her lawyers said.

Her counsel acknowledged that twelve-plus years of unresolved trauma had taken a toll on Constand. The lasting impact of the assault had been detrimental on her relationships with family members and friends, and it had negatively curtailed her career as well. What her counsel needed was a way of measuring this impact and understanding its cumulative effect on her mental health.

They also acknowledged the likelihood that Cosby's lawyer—following the footsteps of pretty much all defense lawyers in cases of sexual assault—would turn issues of memory and trauma into a theater of disdain. To get ahead of this, Constand's lawyers thought it best to hire a consulting expert. That was where I came in. My job would be to administer a psychiatric examination, to get a big-picture understanding of Constand's mental state, and to map out connections between Constand's current psychological well-being and the trauma she experienced at the hands of Bill Cosby back in 2004.

I immediately agreed to help. I just had one caveat: I wanted Constand to have the opportunity to request and receive follow-up counseling sessions with me or with anyone she chose.

"These types of examinations can trigger a lot of strong emotions," I explained. "It's important that she has an outlet of support afterwards."

Constand flew from her home in Canada to Boston later that

same week. Since her trip was only scheduled to last a few hours, I reserved a private conference room at the airport's hotel. I wanted the setting to be as convenient and stress-free as possible, ensuring that Constand could feel safe and comfortable given the subjects we'd inevitably discuss.

"I'm glad we're meeting today," I said, as the two of us took our seats at an oval-shaped table. "As you know, the purpose of this session is for me to conduct a psychiatric examination and write up a report on your mental health. Is that something I have your permission to do?"

Constand, who was dressed in loose-fitting clothing—the type of gray athletic gear someone might wear with the intent of going unnoticed—gave me a look of uncertainty. It struck me as such a disconnect. For a woman who easily cleared six feet, she looked small and vulnerable as she tucked herself into her seat.

"I like to ask permission before starting an exam," I clarified, my voice softening. "This is your choice. It's up to you whether this conversation moves forward or not. *You're* the one in control here."

After a brief hesitation, Constand nodded and said, "Sure," curls of brown hair bobbing around her face. "If that's the case, then yes. It's...it's not easy to talk about, but I believe this is the right thing to do."

"Okay." I clicked my pen and looked down at a blank sheet of paper. "Let's start back in 2004. We'll talk about what happened during the incident itself later. But for now, let's start with the aftermath. Tell me about everything that came after you woke up. How did you feel?"

"Surreal," she said. "Everything felt surreal."

She described waking up the morning after her assault at 4:00 a.m. and just wanting to go home. "I grabbed my things and walked towards the front door. But he was right there—Cosby was. He was standing at the bottom of the staircase, dressed in a robe. He gave me a muffin and said, 'All right,' as if he were trying to reassure me or something. But I just left. I didn't say anything. I just left."

Constand added that initially, she felt too overwhelmed with fear and embarrassment to report the crime. And so instead, she drove home, showered, got dressed, and went to work. She couldn't make sense of what happened. She didn't even want to *think* about it. But it kept nagging at her, and ultimately, she felt a need to confront Cosby about what he'd done.

It took a few days until she finally managed to work up the courage to call him and ask if they could meet up. There was some back-and-forth—he wanted to meet at a restaurant surrounded by a large group, she wanted to meet someplace more private—before Constand agreed to go to his house. When she arrived, Cosby calmly invited her in and led her back to the exact same couch where he'd assaulted her, telling her it was where she'd had an orgasm. She rejected his advances, shutting him down right away. But before she could ask the questions that had been haunting her, she was suddenly struck by a realization: She was powerless in this situation.

Who would ever believe "America's Dad" to be capable of such a gruesome act?

Who would ever trust her word over his?

And so, for the second time, she didn't say anything at all.

She just got up and left.

"I was scared and didn't really know who to turn to," Constand recalled. "I didn't even think of calling the police or running to the hospital because it was such a prominent, wealthy, *famous* person who had done this to me. I just felt silenced. And ashamed."

Constand tried her best to block out the memory and dove headfirst back into her routine, keeping herself busy as the director of women's basketball operations at Temple University. But even that environment reminded her of Cosby. After all, he was a member on the board of trustees. He attended games and often visited campus—a looming presence that made daily life unbearable.

So in the spring of 2004, Constand reluctantly resigned from her job and moved back to her parents' house in Toronto.

Distance, however, wasn't the solution she'd hoped. She began losing weight, she lost interest in sports (once her passion in life), and she frequently screamed herself awake at night. Her parents and sister knew something was wrong. But whenever they tried to talk to Constand about it, she refused to answer. This went on for nearly a year until finally, after a particularly triggering nightmare and premonition that she'd end up dead if she continued holding in her secret, Constand worked up the courage to tell her mom the truth: that Bill Cosby had drugged and raped her.

"It was hard because of all the shame I felt," Constand admitted. "But my mother was the only person I really felt safe with at the time. And, so, you know, we discussed it and she was very, very shocked because Cosby had gotten to know her at the same time as he was getting to know me. He ingratiated himself into my family, calling to check in and sending small gifts. At some points, he even called her 'Mom.' And so, she had his phone number and she called him directly and asked him what he'd done to me, and he basically admitted it. I have no idea why, but he told her about the pills and the assault and everything. At one point, he even said: 'Mom, there was no penile penetration, just digital penetration.' He corroborated everything I'd said."

She paused for a moment and looked out the window, watching planes as they silently rose and receded in the distance.

"Somehow, that made it even *more* awful—that he was so open about it," Constand continued. "Because it showed that he'd been thinking about it, planning it even, and neither me nor my mom had seen it coming."

Despite her outward composure, I began to notice fractures beneath the surface. The conversation was clearly triggering something in Constand—her tone had become mechanical, and her gaze drifted more frequently, staring out the window or the floor or anywhere else to avoid meeting my eyes. The deeper she ventured into her memories, the more detached she became from the present, as if she were slipping into another time, another version of herself.

I had seen this before in survivors of sexual assault. Trauma manifests in different ways for different people, but one underlying feature remains strikingly consistent—the way it fractures a person's sense of self. It creates a split. There's the person who existed before their trauma, and the person who now exists *because* of their trauma. And because trauma is not just remembered but viscerally *relived*, a trigger can pull a survivor back in an instant, forcing them to psychologically reinhabit the very moment they long to escape. In Constand's case, the trigger was thinking back to her final memory before losing consciousness on Cosby's couch. "His hands," she said. "I can still feel his hands on my thighs."

That's the unseen horror of trauma. It's forever. It's chronic.

"I know this is a hard conversation to have," I reassured her, encouraging Constand as best I could, "but that's what makes it so important. Pain is part of the healing process. I've seen too many victims try to make themselves numb after a traumatic event. It seems natural, right? That desire to block out the world when you can't protect your physical boundaries? But it's the worst thing you can do. It creates this massive buildup of emotions that seeps out as mental health issues or physically debilitating disease. When left unchecked, trauma can wreak havoc on your life, consuming you entirely."

We took a break so that Constand could collect herself and create a bit of separation from the immediacy that trauma memories impose. She stretched a little, which I think helped her feel more grounded. And when we came back, she was refocused and ready to continue. She went on to tell me that her mom had encouraged her to go to the police to file a report. The idea had initially terrified her—understandably so. Who wouldn't be terrified? Opening up to family was one thing, but the idea of opening up to strangers was something *entirely* different. On top of that, she had little faith the authorities would believe her. Still, at her mother's encouragement she agreed to go anyway, and she launched her official complaint with the Cheltenham Township Police Station in Pennsylvania on January 18, 2005.

"I remember speaking with the police and having that feeling of, like, 'This report I'm making must be really unbelievable to them.' Because, you know, Bill Cosby was America's Dad at the time. He was still touring, and doing all his comedy routines, and he was active in the community, too. He still had that clout. I did it, though, and it was a very daunting process, but I got through it okay and I had my family's support. And I think that was one of the positives at the time; it was that I didn't feel so alone. I felt like I had my mother and my family, and I had a really good support system."

Upon hearing Constand's complaint, the police immediately opened an investigation. A media frenzy followed suit, but the coverage was largely skeptical of Constand's story. *Why now?* every article seemed to imply. The not-so-subtle subtext? *What's her motivation? Could it be financial gain?* But that was just boilerplate laziness. Delayed reporting is a very real thing, especially when the victim feels there's a lot at stake, as was the case here. And whether the media wants to believe it or not, celebrities are just as capable of criminal behavior as anyone else. The only difference is that they have greater resources to get away with it.

"My whole personal life unfolded after that. I wasn't really thinking about it at the time—how big a can of worms I was opening by reporting this—but everything got pretty crazy pretty fast. And that was challenging. Because, you know, nobody wants to be famous for being sexually assaulted."

As part of the investigation, Cosby agreed to participate in an interview at his attorney's midtown Manhattan law office. He wore one of his signature Cliff Huxtable sweaters for the occasion, actively answering questions and making an overall impression on Cheltenham police chief John Norris of being "cooperative, congenial." But other officers walked away feeling less convinced.

When asked whether he'd engaged in "penile penetration" with Constand, Cosby hesitated, then responded: "Never asleep or awake." It was an odd remark, to say the least, with some officers describing it as evasive.

Despite this and other ongoing concerns, the investigation only lasted a short number of weeks before being shut down by District Attorney Bruce Castor, who formally announced that charges would not be filed due to "insufficient credible and admissible evidence." Cosby's lawyers were quick to follow suit with a statement of their own. They wholeheartedly denied Constand's allegations, dismissing them as "preposterous"—a word choice that seemed strange considering Cosby's prior track record of sexual misconduct allegations. And yet the whole thing went unquestioned by the media. Clearly there was a pattern to Cosby's behaviors, but neither the judiciary nor the public was ready to listen.

Disappointed but undeterred, Constand lodged a civil suit against Cosby for battery and assault in July 2015. This change of tack came at the suggestion of her legal team. The criminal charges weren't leading anywhere. With a civil suit, though, there was a chance for Constand to find at least some degree of restitution. The filing included depositions from thirteen other women, all of whom made similar statements about how Cosby had pressured them with pills and alcohol before sexually assaulting them.

"I wanted criminal justice. I wanted to see him held accountable for what he did to me. I wanted to see him go to *jail*," Constand stressed. "But the district attorney at the time, Bruce Castor, said there just wasn't enough credible evidence and that both of us, both Cosby *and* I, would come across in some sort of negative light. So the only option I really had after that was to pursue a civil case against him."

During the four days that he sat for deposition, Cosby spoke at great length about his extramarital affairs. He testified to his habit of drugging women with quaaludes to get them to have sex with him, of using his celebrity status to stop allegations from surfacing, of hiding the affairs from his wife, and of sending hush money to pay off multiple victims. He was eerily open and honest and answered every question he was asked. But he didn't do this in good faith. He did this because he thought he was protected. His lawyers told him that the deposition would be sealed, which was unusual given that most depositions are public information. But Cosby, fully trusting the most powerful lawyers money could buy, assumed none of this would ever see the light of day.

Hearing these admissions was a shock for Constand. It must have been a shock for Cosby's lawyers, too, because right after that, the suit was quietly settled and bound by a nondisclosure agreement. Almost as quickly as the session was finished, the deposition was sealed. Everything Constand heard would have to stay tightly locked up in her head.

"I went in there with a secret, and I came out of there with a secret," Constand said bitterly. "Cosby had been drugging women for *years*."

"That was his strategy," I replied, remembering all that I'd read about allegations against him in the past. "He knew that if he could get his victims in an unconscious state or an altered state of consciousness, that would give him an advantage to always say, 'Oh, you must have been dreaming' or 'Nothing really happened.' He was protecting himself in the event that any of his crimes ever made it to court. The fact that his victims had been drugged would make them seem unreliable to a judge, to a jury."

"I should never have signed the nondisclosure agreement," Constand said, her tone full of regret. "I let Cosby take away my voice."

———

In the end, it wasn't one of Cosby's victims who galvanized his downfall—it was a fellow entertainer. During a live show in Philadelphia in October 2014, comedian Hannibal Buress criticized Cosby for being a hypocritical moralist who assaulted and raped women. He told the audience to google accusations of rape against Cosby. So the audience did. And when a short video of Buress's show went viral across social media, countless others googled the accusations as well.

"That video just rocked my world," Constand remembered. "I was getting ready to go to bed that night, and I looked on Facebook and one of my friends had posted the video. I felt...it was kind of like an earthquake under my feet, to be honest with you, because I thought if people went and googled 'Bill Cosby rape,' they were going to find my name, too."

The next morning, Constand's phone buzzed incessantly, flooded with people reaching out to ask if she'd seen the video, if she was okay, if there was anything she needed. These gestures were likely well-meaning. But to Constand, the sudden wave of attention felt intrusive. She thought that she'd moved on from that part of her life. And yet here it was, resurfaced, tearing open old wounds and leaving them raw, exposed, and festering in the harsh light of day.

As Constand withdrew further into herself, the Hannibal Buress video spread further and further outward. Each share, like, and comment added new momentum to the video's viral advance, propelling it into a broader cultural conversation. Lines were drawn. Fellow entertainers took sides, adding their voices to the court of public opinion. This surge of interest compelled the media to cover the story more closely than they had back in 2004. Public sentiment had forced their hand.

And the impact didn't end with the media.

The video's virality had unintentionally prompted more and more victims to come forward and share their stories. It inspired *courage*. Now, in addition to the original thirteen Jane Does from Constand's civil suit against Cosby, there was a total of twenty, then thirty, then thirty-five women who stood up to face him. By July 2015, *New York* magazine was running a feature story, profiling thirty-five of Cosby's accusers and their stories of assault. The magazine's cover pictured the women sitting side by side in four rows, with a thirty-sixth seat left empty, symbolically representing the victims who were still unable to come forward.

Several universities stripped Cosby of his honorary degrees. Brown University, for one, put out the following statement: "It has become clear by his own admission in legal depositions that became public this summer, that Mr. Cosby has engaged in conduct with women that is contrary to the values of Brown and the qualities for which he was honored by the university in 1985."

Other institutions and former colleagues took steps to distance themselves from Cosby as well.

With public pressure mounting, the Associated Press filed a motion to have Cosby's deposition in Constand's civil suit unsealed.

A U.S. district judge agreed to the request, citing that the deposition offered a "stark contrast" to Cosby's identity as a "public moralist." Immediately after the deposition was released, newspapers across the world printed Cosby's own damning words, talking all about how he used drugs and fame to sexually pursue women against their will.

In one particularly revealing section of the deposition, a lawyer asked Cosby straight out, "When you got the quaaludes, was it in your mind that you were going to use these quaaludes for young women that you wanted to have sex with?"

To this, Cosby responded with a single word: "Yes."

———

I looked toward the window. Low-angled sunlight was gleaming, reflected by a row of stationary planes. I hadn't noticed how late it was getting. Constand, who was visibly exhausted at this point in our conversation, must have realized how late it was getting, too. She skipped forward in her retelling to December 2015.

"It was one week before the statute of limitations would expire on my case," Constand explained. "December thirtieth, that's when I formally filed charges against Cosby for assaulting me back in 2004."

Cosby's lawyers were quick to frame the whole thing as a smear campaign: "Mr. Cosby is no stranger to discrimination and racial hatred... When the media repeats her accusations—with no evidence, no trial and no jury—we are moved backwards as a country and away from the America that our civil rights leaders sacrificed so much to create."

"I couldn't understand it," Constand said. "There was all this conversation about me in the media and on CNN...knowing I had a confidential settlement and couldn't defend myself?"

Constand's use of the phrase "couldn't defend myself" stood out to me right away, since it echoed her inability to defend herself against Cosby's sexual advances after being drugged. The basis of Andrea Constand's PTSD symptoms illustrate the neurobiology of a traumatic event on the limbic system. Reminders to the original event—in this case, Bruce Castor's defamatory statements on public television and on Twitter—activated the memory system to the traumatic event again. The stressor involves indirect exposure to aversive details of the trauma.

By this point, I had no doubt that Constand had been assaulted, but that wasn't the entirety of the question at stake here. I needed to figure out if Constand would be able to withstand the intense media scrutiny that would come with such a public trial, even more so than she faced now. So I asked her about how she felt on December 31, 2015—the day Cosby was officially charged with three counts of indecent sexual assault.

"Terrified," she admitted. "I realized that there were going to be a lot of things outside my control."

Even so, Constand acknowledged the value of getting a second shot at justice. It was a rare opportunity—not only to hold Cosby accountable for herself, but for dozens of other women as well.

"That's part of why I'm meeting with you," Constand told me. "There's no real winning for me at this point. I've lost in every way there is. But I can do something good here by preparing for trial, understanding the tactics his lawyers will use, and making sure that I'm there and comfortable and present. All I can do is tell the truth, and the truth will be my power."

I'd gathered enough information to write my report, so I followed Constand's lead and turned my attention to trial strategies.

"Yes," I said, "but the defense will try to diminish your truth by attacking your character and portraying you as unreliable. They'll try to poke holes in your motivation, memory, and intent. They'll do everything they can to get under your skin. They want you to slip up in front of the jury, so they'll make their attacks personal."

"This *is* personal."

"I know it is. And that's part of what makes testifying so hard," I said. "You have to separate yourself from all those personal feelings and keep your focus on the jury. *They're* the ones who make the final decision at trial. It's important that they make their decision based on truth, rather than emotion. So it's up to you to share your truth, your story, your experience that only you know and lived."

Constand thought about this for a moment, seriously considering every word.

"I'm not sure I can do that," she hedged. "It's been ten years, but talking about it still feels very raw to me."

"You can't expect to be perfect," I told her. "The best you can do is be prepared."

I went on to explain that Cosby's lawyers would likely take a standard approach. Just like the general public, juries often know very little—if anything at *all*—about trauma and sexual assault. Cosby's lawyers would use this to their advantage. They'd probably make a big deal of Constand's delayed reporting, but fail to provide the context that delayed reporting was statistically more the norm than the exception in cases of sexual assault. They'd also likely claim that Cosby and Constand's prior relationship was proof of consent, but fail to explain that the majority of sexual assault cases are committed by someone who knows the victim. They'd also probably dredge up the 2005 civil suit and subsequent settlement as a way of framing Constand, but they'd conveniently fail to mention her ten years of adhering to the nondisclosure agreement, or acknowledge that Cosby had been the one to break the terms of their deal. And they'd do all of this because it had a high chance of working. The odds were in their favor. Since the mid-1970s, the data surrounding sexual assault cases hadn't really changed: Of all the cases reported to police in a given year, only 8 percent result in the perpetrator going to jail.

"They'll pathologize you," I warned her. "They'll say *you're* the problem. They'll reduce you to nothing more than an unavoidable by-product of male success. That's the myth you're battling. All the old tropes and stigmas against victims of assault are still there: *She asked for it. It's because of how she was dressed. It's because of this or that or whatever excuse seems most convenient.* It's the same thing *every time*. They'll blame *you* before blaming the offender. And it might even start to feel that way while you're up there on the stand, listening to whatever twisted narrative the defense is trying to weave.

"It might even feel like you're at fault," I continued. "But it's important to remember that you're not. Nothing you said or did could *ever* justify Cosby's actions. And you deserve justice. *That's* the only thing that matters."

CHAPTER 8

Accountability

I saw Constand in a different light once our four-hour conversation was over. She looked frailer as she stood up. Exhausted, to be sure, but a little unburdened, too. And it was because of everything she'd poured into our conversation that I now had a firm understanding of who she was, the trauma she'd experienced, and the extent of the psychological damages she'd suffered. Let me be clear: These weren't opinions I'd formed; they were clinical observations I'd gathered by conducting a trauma-informed mental health assessment that allowed me to measure and describe the specific nature of Constand's trauma, both its origins and effects. And to be even clearer, yes, psychological damages can be quantified despite their "invisible" nature. Because regardless of the reflexive stigma that surrounds issues of psychological pain here in the United States, its existence is just as real as a broken bone, pneumonia, or a sprained knee.

My assessment had two immediate impacts. First, it was

validating for Constand to be heard by a professional. She'd been heard by friends and family and lawyers, of course. But that's different. There's bias there, since the intent is usually to provide understanding and comfort. In my capacity, though, I wasn't listening with any preconceived notions or desired outcomes in mind. I was listening for the truth, and what I heard confirmed the existence and magnitude of her trauma, a brutal reality that many others had dismissed as "all in your head." That was huge—to finally be *believed* after years of second guessing.

But the assessment had an even bigger impact as far as the legal team was concerned. They were facing a near-impossible task of building a case around no forensic evidence, no witnesses, no additional victim accounts, and no real prospects beyond a classic showdown of he-said-she-said. Given the limitations—and the fact that years of investigative data show that it's overwhelmingly unlikely for sexual assault cases to end in conviction—the team had wrestled with considerable doubts about the viability of moving forward at all. My assessment changed all that. As an expert, my assessment was concrete evidence that would stand up in the court of law.

Of course, legal battles are bound by parity. And so I knew I wouldn't be the only expert consultant meeting with Constand, since the defense would hire a consultant of their own. That person would need to interview Constand in order to write a psychiatric evaluation based on their own knowledge and experience. Both of our reports would then become part of the trial's public record, which meant that the defense would have an opportunity to see and challenge my analysis in open court, but *also* that I'd have an opportunity to see and challenge theirs.

As I've always said, expert analysis has the power to make or break a case. This is something I've never taken for granted. Even though the back-and-forth exchanges between experts and legal counsel are only a small piece within the greater complexity of a trial, the ripple effects from these exchanges can sometimes change the verdict itself.

After submitting my initial assessment to Constand's legal team, it took me several more weeks to write up a comprehensive psychiatric evaluation that would stand up to the rigors of trial. This was because I'd intentionally used both qualitative and quantitative techniques during the interview. Now that I'd had some time to process and step back, I wanted to analyze each set of data on its own, and then contextualize these results by stitching them together so that one could support the other to paint a complete picture of Constand's mental health. This allowed me to be as objective as possible. It was how I mapped out my evaluation process, how I double-checked my own work.

I started by taking a closer look at the qualitative aspects of the data. These were heavily focused on a range of sensory specific perceptions—sight, sound, touch, smell, and so on—that had become embedded within and inseparable from Constand's memory of how her trauma occurred. In fact, these sensory recollections were directly linked to how trauma manifested itself after a particular incident. For example, if a victim was attacked at a crowded party at night, they might exhibit behavioral symptoms, such as difficulty sleeping or withdrawal from social settings, or even psychological symptoms, including guilt, anger, or flashbacks. Regardless, these responses were involuntary and were characterized by their vivid "nowness," popping up and taking over as if the trauma were happening all over again—unable to be controlled or shut off.

The qualitative part of my analysis involved pulling various case documents to verify the details of the victim's account. Even though I valued my interview with Constand and believed she was telling the truth as best she could, it was still important for me to do my own independent research rather than simply accept her story at face value. Victims—through no fault of their own—often misremember details. This is normal. Repression, memory fragmentation, distortion—these are just some of the ways the brain tries to protect us from our prior trauma. But as normal and self-protective as this is, it meant there was also a possibility of gaps in Constand's recollection. In this case, I requested a variety of documentation to corroborate her account, including a copy of the civil complaint, her deposition from 2016, counseling notes by Constand's therapists, and a representative sample of all the hate mail and internet bullying she'd been subjected to over the last several months.

To round out my evaluation, I also included the results of two well-known and highly regarded clinical surveys I'd administered to Constand toward the end of our interview. The first was the Beck Depression Index, a series of twenty-one questions created by psychiatrist Aaron T. Beck, first published back in 1961, that measure characteristic attitudes and symptoms of depression, whether that's physical symptoms like weight loss and fatigue, or psychiatric symptoms like hopelessness and guilt.

The second survey was the Impact of Event Scale, a twenty-two-item questionnaire designed to measure subjective distress caused by traumatic events. This survey is predicated on the idea that until traumatic experiences are psychologically assimilated, the victim is trapped in a loop of intrusive thoughts in one moment and then quickly toggles to disassociation and avoidance strategies in the next. By measuring the frequency and scale of an individual's distress, the survey acts as a useful tool for understanding the overall degree of trauma. Both surveys lent additional credibility to my overall assessment. I was fairly confident that the defense team's consulting expert might be tempted to dismiss my background or individual analysis, but it would be a lot harder for them to dismiss these two evidence-based surveys on top of that.

Ultimately, my report followed a standardized format I'd developed over the course of several years: a biographical summary of the subject; an outline of how the subject saw herself; the administration and outcome of mental health exams; notes and analysis of supplemental counseling notes from therapists; my opinions and basis for those opinions; and finally, a summary of my overall assessment. My main takeaway was that Constand had indeed been sexually assaulted by Bill Cosby, and consequently suffered from chronic posttraumatic stress disorder. Furthermore, I believed that these trauma-specific symptoms—that is, anxiety, intrusive thoughts, avoidance—were a permanent, neurobiological response to an unnatural or extreme event. In other words, trauma had caused an irreversible shift in Constand's brain and nervous system.

My report wasn't about choosing sides, then picking out evidence to support some sort of preformed conclusion. It was about mapping out the methodological process I'd used to reach an unbiased opinion of Constand's experience, grounded in decades of established practice. I felt strongly enough about this fact that in every report I wrote, I included this line: "All of my opinions herein are stated within a reasonable degree of psychiatric nursing and nursing sciences certainty."

I submitted my report to the court in March 2017. Copies went to all the various trial constituents, including the defense, who'd selected a Philadelphia-area psychiatrist as their consulting expert. The defense expert's meeting with Constand took place at his office in Bryn Mawr, Pennsylvania, on September 1, 2017. And within just three days, his report was written up, submitted, and added to the trial's official record.

I was surprised to see the defense expert's report submitted so quickly. Three days was a quick turnaround for a case as complex as Constand's. Typically, a well-constructed report takes several weeks. There were other surprises in my initial reading of the report, too, beginning with the substantially shorter length of the psychiatric evaluation itself, "two and a quarter hours," and the defense expert's decision to supplement his evaluation by administering the Minnesota Multiphasic Personality Inventory-2 questionnaire (MMPI-2)—a 567 true-false self-reporting tool designed to assist clinicians in the diagnosis of mental disorders.

But perhaps most surprising was that the defense expert's report *started* with a conclusion: the MMPI-2 report, stating that Ms. Constand's profile "is within the normal range." This was a red flag for me. It felt biased—like he'd started with exactly the opinion the defense had hired him to find and then worked his way backward, justifying his foregone conclusion from one page to the next. I was also dismayed by the expert's choice to implement the MMPI-2 in the first place since numerous peer-reviewed studies showed MMPI-2 to be far less reliable at diagnosing PTSD in victims of sexual assault than in combat veterans. It was clear to me that if the defense expert genuinely wanted to assess Constand's psychiatric condition, he was using the wrong tool for the job.

Next up, the defense expert's report included ten pages of excerpts from external documents: records from Constand's therapists and the hospital, the deposition transcript, and my psychiatric report. But that was it—just excerpts, without any context at all. No insights, no rationale, no analysis of the defense expert's own; there were simply ten pages of cut-and-pasted text, followed by eight additional pages of stand-alone quotes taken from Constand's conversations with other professionals. The only written contribution from the defense expert was a series of all-caps headers that screamed: "HISTORY FROM MS. CONSTAND RELATED TO CURRENT CLAIM," "PAST MEDICAL HISTORY FROM MS. CONSTAND," "FAMILY HISTORY FROM MS. CONSTAND," "PSYCHIATRIC HISTORY FROM MS. CONSTAND," "SUBSTANCE USE HISTORY FROM MS. CONSTAND," and so on.

I read the defense expert's assessment twice on the off chance I'd missed something essential. Some sort of rationale or evidence that justified its foregone conclusion. But, it was anyone's guess as to why these particular excerpts had been chosen or what evaluative purpose they were intended to convey.

And maybe that was the point.

Maybe the defense expert knew *exactly* what he was doing by taking such a hands-off approach. After all, it's rare for sexual assault cases to resolve in the victim's favor. Add to that the obvious weaknesses of the case—the event took place twelve years ago, delayed reporting to the police, Cosby's previously paid financial settlement—and any of these factors could lead the jury to find reasonable doubt. It would be easiest, then, for the defense expert to simply follow the path of least resistance. To stand out of the way of a legal system that's disproportionately stacked against survivors who speak out. To enable victim-blaming, cultural bias, and stereotypes to prevail yet again. He would know that jurors often have an aversion to identifying with the victim. All *he* had to do was validate this preconditioned way of thinking by typecasting Constand as just another hysterical woman who refused to take accountability for a consensual relationship she'd now come to regret.

Because the defense expert's report had followed mine, he directly rebutted my claims, arguing that he disagreed with my opinion of chronic posttraumatic stress disorder or the possibility that Constand suffered from depression or any other kind of psychiatric disorder following the incident. However, whereas I'd used my report to lay out the scientific reasoning behind my evaluations, the defense expert's justifications leaned more on those preexisting patriarchal norms, summing up his thoughts by saying, "[Constand] appears to be reasonably happy with her current lifestyle."

I remember reading this and thinking, *Really? She appears*

reasonably happy? How much more surface level could a clinical report get?

Altogether, there was really nothing in those twenty-six pages that revealed anything significant to me about Constand. But they revealed *plenty* about the defense expert himself.

It took me about a month to write up my official response to the defense expert's report, which I submitted on October 14. My goal was to clarify the rationale behind how I made my evaluation in the first place, the scientific principles and methods and standards I'd employed. It's the jury's job to evaluate evidence and the facts of the case for themselves as objectively as possible, and I needed them to see my process so they could trust that my assessment would help them do just that.

Beyond that, I felt strongly that the defense expert's report ignored basic fundamentals about the nature of PTSD itself. In his report, the expert asserted that Constand had not experienced "events that would meet the DSM-5 definition of traumatic events." But since PTSD is rooted in neurobiology, it's very possible for subsequent events an individual experiences to reactivate the primary disorder. In fact, reactivation of PTSD has been observed in clinical literature relating to civilian survivors of war, the Holocaust, and sexual trauma.* In Constand's case, newfound media attention and the remarks by Mr. Castor brought back all the past memories of the Cosby incident. And reactivation doesn't always look the same for everyone who suffers from PTSD, either. For some people, trauma can be somewhat self-contained in the

---

* Kinzie et al., 2002.

form of sleep disturbances or heightened sensitivity to sudden noise. For other people, it can be wholly life altering—a constant barrage of panic attacks, flashbacks, and self-destructive behaviors.

The second point I focused on in my response was the defense expert's conclusion: "Ms. Constand does not have PTSD, depression, or any other psychiatric disorder at present." I found this odd given that the defense expert's report itself included many examples that served to support a diagnosis of PTSD and also of a reactivation of PTSD due to current circumstances. For example, it described Constand as happy in one sentence, then anxious in the next. As social, then isolated. Confident, but full of negative thoughts. On and on, the report was full of self-contradictions.

The basis of Andrea Constand's PTSD symptoms illustrate the neurobiology of a traumatic event on the limbic system. Reminders to the original event, in this case Bruce Castor's hurtful public statements on public television and on Twitter, activated the memory system to the traumatic event again. As she told the defense expert, "Why is he [Bruce Castor] doing this? Why is he talking about me on CNN...knowing I had a confidential settlement and couldn't defend myself?" This statement of not being able to defend herself replicates her inability to defend herself against the sexual acts by Bill Cosby because of being drugged.

I ended my response by reiterating the fact that Constand had indeed experienced increased anxiety, hyperarousal, and resultant chest pains since hearing the hurtful public comments made by Mr. Castor, knowing they would exist online forever. It wasn't just that Ms. Constand was "unhappy" about this. Rather, her reputation had been directly attacked in a public forum, and she'd received scores of threats, hate mail, and unwanted media attention, all which combined to reactivate the chronic posttraumatic stress disorder that she'd initially suffered from the sexual assault by Bill Cosby. She'd been assaulted. She'd been violated. And all of this had left very real psychological scars.

———

I met with Constand once more before the trial. Our conversation was an extension of the first: primarily, I listened and offered counseling. I also did what I could to help her prepare for the spectacle ahead. What was different this time around was that the judge presiding over the case had ruled it permissible for evidence of Cosby's "prior bad acts"—a nuanced and subjectively applied legal code in Pennsylvania—to be presented at trial.

As it's written, the bad acts code states that "evidence of a person's character or character trait is not admissible to prove that on a particular occasion the person acted in accordance with the character or trait." In simpler terms, the rule is intended to block prosecutors from introducing evidence that reduces a defendant to a generically bad person, which could potentially factor into a jury's prejudice regarding the defendant's innocence or guilt. But bad act evidence *is* allowed if it serves to show "motive, opportunity, intent, preparation, plan, knowledge, identity, absence of mistake, or lack of accident." In Cosby's case, his repeated nature of drugging and assaulting women, and the consistency of claims from the dozens of victims who came forward, was all deemed relevant to present to the jury.

This decision was a *huge* advantage for the prosecution.

In all likelihood, it would seal Cosby's fate.

"The whole he-said-she-said thing doesn't feel so insurmountable anymore," Constand said to me afterward. She then told me about a podcast she'd recently listened to where the host read out "he said" and "she said" statements for each of Cosby's victims.

"It was so powerful," she told me. "It really just drove home the point that I'm not doing this on my own anymore."

"That will be important to remember when the trial starts," I said.

"You think it will be that bad?" she asked.

"Not bad, exactly," I said after a moment. "Lonely. And a little vulnerable in a way. That's the nature of these things. The defense will try to discredit you. They'll try to make you feel isolated and confused. They'll try to shape a narrative where you can't even trust yourself."

"How?"

"By doing everything they can to discredit you. The playbook hasn't changed much over the years. It's always the same three-pronged attack: they'll say the relationship was consensual, they'll highlight any inconsistences in your memory of the assault, and they'll say you're making the whole thing up to gain some sort of advantage."

"Doesn't sound much different than the last ten years of my life," Constand said, half making a joke.

"That's a good perspective to have," I reassured her. "Try to hold on to that, to not get caught up in the moment. Because here's the thing: I've seen over and over again how infuriatingly easy it is for an attorney to take someone's experience with sexual aggression and recast it as romance. They'll argue that you accepted his invitation to come over and insinuate you were try-ing to get something out of the relationship, as if you brought the whole thing upon yourself. But you *didn't*. And *none* of this is your fault. If anything, it's an indictment on how our culture nor-malizes skewed relationship dynamics between men and women. How there's a tacit excuse that enables men, especially men in power, to casually and habitually engage in inappropriate behav-iors towards women, knowing full well that women tend to put up with it—at least in the short term—since that's easier than pushing back. In other words, the challenge you'll face is being implicated as complicit in your own attack for no other reason than that you were there and attacked in the first place. That's the warped reality you're up against. It's victim blaming. Guilty until proven innocent."

———

After six days and fifty-two hours of debate, the twelve-person jury on Cosby's criminal sexual-assault trial ended in deadlock on June 19, 2017. The presiding judge accepted the defense's motion for a mistrial, telling the court that the outcome represented "nei-ther a vindication nor a victory" for either side.

I, for one, felt frustrated, since it seemed like the decision had everything to do with the legal process and nothing to do with actually serving justice. After all, *both* parties agreed that Cosby pressured Constand into taking three pills he identified obscurely as "friends." *Both* parties agreed that Constand became very sleepy after taking these pills. And *both* parties agreed that Cosby then physically penetrated Constand before leaving her unconscious and partially undressed on a sofa in his Pennsylvania house. Given all this, it made no sense that the jury was mired in deadlock.

But there was something about the overt disparity of this outcome that still had an impact on our culture at large. This was a high-profile case of the greatest magnitude. Every single moment had been chronicled and commented on and broadcast throughout the entire spectrum of media, unlike any sexual assault case before. It was impossible for the public to unsee such flagrant abuse of power and privilege.

Regardless of whether or not Cosby was going to face jail time, this trial represented a tipping point, a foreshadowing of what was to come for others, like him, who had abused their positions of power. Cosby's legacy was now in tatters. Even his self-satisfied exit down the courthouse handicapped ramp—his publicist on one side, his lawyer on the other raising a fist in solidarity toward the press—seemed tense and less than celebratory.

A storm was coming.

You could feel it building up slowly but surely, like an electrical charge zapping through the air.

Immediately after the announcement of a mistrial, Montgomery County district attorney Kevin R. Steele publicly stated his intention to retry the case, which in turn set off a series of culturally connected events. The first occurred just a few months later, on October 5, 2017, when the *New York Times* ran the front-page headline "Sexual Misconduct Claims Trail a Hollywood Mogul." The accompanying article shined a light on numerous sexual-abuse allegations against Harvey Weinstein, one of the entertainment industry's most powerful and untouchable men at the time. For a long-time advocate for sexual assault victims like me, it was an amazing thing to witness—both the sheer number of claims and the investigative integrity with which they were being handled. The tone and tenor of these conversations felt different, too. Victims were now generally supported by the public, not shunned, and subsequently felt empowered to come forward. This led to *more* accusations against other high-profile men, *more* voices speaking out. And as one victim after another found the courage to step out from the darkness, the movement expanded outward—all these concentric circles of light joining together to cut through the stigma and bias and widespread culture of abuse that had felt insurmountable for far too long.

For Constand, this revolution of public perception culminated one year later, when her retrial ended with a verdict she'd been denied for more than a decade. At long last, Cosby was found guilty. Ultimately, he was convicted of three felony counts of aggravated indecent assault: penetration without consent, penetration while the victim was unconscious, and penetration after administering an intoxicant. The judge designated Cosby a "sexually violent predator" and sentenced him to state prison for a period of "no less than three years and no more than ten years." The eighty-one-year-old Cosby would have to register as a sex offender and bear the weight of that public disgrace for the rest of his life.

It would be difficult to overstate the significance of this verdict. Far more than simply a shift in the balance of power, it was as if an entirely new landscape had emerged for victims of sexual assault. And although no single spark ignited this cultural sea, Constand, through pain and persistence, became an early emblem for what eventually evolved into the #MeToo movement. Her case had galvanized and inspired a nation, proving that a victim *could* demand accountability despite even the greatest asymmetry of power. Through sheer will, Constand managed to recalibrate the scales of justice, giving hope to fellow survivors.

That's no small thing.

That's *everything*.

The ripple effect of Constand's work continues to impact the world in significant ways. She's become a fierce advocate for fellow victims, an inspiration to many, and she goes out of her way twice a year to speak to my class and to humanize her experience for my students. During one of those visits, she described trauma in a way that I'll never forget:

"It's like a really bad scar over a painful injury. It's this living tissue that forms pathways in your brain and makes it hard to remember details. That's how I experienced it, and it's why I made some mistakes in my police statements, which is something I've always openly acknowledged and admit even in court when the defense team tried to turn it against me. But that's my reality. And it's the reality for a lot of people who, for whatever reason, are forced to remember an experience of trauma they've tried to forget for so long. None of it's perfect. And so coming forward and kind of stepping into that, I tried to take ownership of that and not let it be turned against me. And that's a really, really difficult thing. But it's just how trauma works. And so I've had to grow into that way of thinking, that way of understanding. Like, this is normal. And that's the lesson, really. The scar is part of having trauma. It proves that the trauma is really there."

Constand is right: Trauma, assault, violence—these are culture-sized problems that require culture-sized solutions. They take a wholesale shift in understanding, something I'd been battling for my entire career. Constand was the tipping point. She brought about a type of cultural revolution unlike anything I'd seen before.

Finally, the floodgates were open.

CHAPTER 9

Kemper Revisited

It always stuck with me—that feeling of being an outsider. Despite my success in criminal profiling, victimology, high-stakes courtroom testimony, and everything else I'd achieved throughout my career, I never quite shook the sense of being on the outside looking in.

Of course, I never made those feelings known. That would only make things worse. And so, for years I navigated my outsiderness by performing a look of ease and pretending it didn't matter. I'd simply register the feeling, then rationalize it away as nothing more than an inevitability of timing—a symptom of being a woman whose career coincided with the height of the second-wave feminism movement.

For a while, this approach helped, but it had very little real-world effect. There was still the practical matter of having to prove myself each and every day, just to reset and do it all over again the next. It was a burden. It was a whole lot of effort wasted on simply trying to blend in.

So I stopped.

Because the truth is it *did* matter. My experience as an outsider was integral to who I was—who I've always been and will always be. It was the landscape that had shaped me and a major reason why I excelled at my career. I'd met brilliant minds at the FBI and within academia, to be sure, but they were constrained by bottom lines, group-think, and the great institutional necessity of "managing up." Outsiders have the freedom to subvert all that. We can choose our own path without the burden of having to explain what we're doing or why. And besides, when you really cut to the heart of it, who wants to be an insider when there are mavericks out there whose visionary ideas can change the world?

I met Gregory Horoupian through an email in November 2018. He introduced himself as a filmmaker who'd spent years researching serial killer Edmund Kemper. He'd recently come across a presentation of mine that included never-before-seen video footage of an interview between Kemper and the FBI. Greg wrote:

> I believe the clip was from the 1988 International Homicide Symposium hosted at Quantico by Bob Ressler. I had submitted a FOIPA request to the FBI for this video, and the subsequent response was that:... *the potentially responsive records were not in their expected location and could not be located...* Since the FBI seems to have misplaced their copy, and since you seem to have access to the 1988 IHS, I'm hoping you can point me towards the right contact to pursue finding this footage in viewable form [emphasis in original].

Greg's email caught my attention right away. I was used to copy-and-paste style media requests from newscasters and production companies looking to retell the same oversensationalized story of my work developing profiling for the BSU. But here was someone who'd mentioned the 1988 IHS by name. He'd clearly done his research. And his line about the FBI misplacing their copy was funny, too.

Still, I was hesitant. My copy of the 1988 IHS was, in all likelihood, the last one left. And with the exception of those few short clips from my presentation, no recording of the tape had ever passed beyond Quantico's hallowed walls. I wasn't sure what the Bureau would think about me showing it to a filmmaker. But then again, they were the ones who hadn't bothered keeping their copy secure and safe.

I emailed him back saying I'd like to talk.

———

A lot came out of that initial conversation. Greg was excited and animated and had a tendency toward single-mindedness that could rival most academics. He was serious in his interest toward Kemper. But he made a point of saying he wasn't a fan of true crime and that his fascination with Kemper came about unexpectedly.

"It started with a quote," Greg said. "You probably know the one. It's from that first prison interview. The one where [FBI agent John] Douglas goes: 'I would be less than honest if I didn't admit that I liked Ed.'"

"I remember that," I said. "Several of the other agents agreed."

"Okay, wow, I didn't know that. But it makes perfect sense and fits exactly with what caught my attention in the first place—the idea that a federal agent could feel this way about a convicted serial killer. I mean, how is that even possible? Especially for an agent like Douglas, whose job is to go to crime scenes and witness firsthand what someone like Kemper can do. It seems impossible."

"Kemper isn't as simple as the violence of his actions," I replied. "Few serial killers are. I'm sure that seems obvious now, but changing that perception was one of the biggest hurdles we faced early on at the BSU. 'Serial killers are crazy. End of story. Lock 'em up and throw away the key.' Of course, that was nothing more than bias confirmation, and it's since become common knowledge that the deeper you go into their heads, the more complicated they get. But a lot of that only came about because of Kemper and his inherent charm and intelligence, plus the fact that he was also self-aware enough to realize these things and use them to his advantage in how he went after victims. I think that's what John was driving at when he said what he said."

"Mmm-hmm," Greg mused, followed by a staticky shuffle. Then his voice came back saying, "Sorry, I'm just writing this down. It's helpful because a lot of what I've been doing is trying to figure out where the myth ends and where the real Kemper begins. I started with the available books, podcasts, and things like that, but I realized they were full of inconsistencies. And then the more I worked my way backwards, the more I saw Kemper's story shift. It was like a game of telephone where the goal was to up the level of sensationalism with each retelling."

"People love a good monster story," I agreed.

"I get it, but don't you think that's strange?" he asked. "I mean, it's not like I don't understand the fascination with serial killers. But they're only fascinating because they're real—because there's not much separating them from us. Kemper is basically just a myth. His story's been so overembellished and misreported and amended over the years that it's hardly even real anymore. It's become more about the storytellers than what actually happened. And I feel like that's a problem. Because what's the point of even telling his story unless you tell it as faithfully as possible? How else can you hold him accountable to his crimes?

"Like, just take the simple example where everyone says he was born weighing thirteen pounds. Even his Wikipedia page says that. But it's wrong. His birth documents show he weighed eight pounds, six ounces when he was born. And like I said, it's a simple example, but things like that add to the myth and makes it easy to dismiss his accountability by saying he was born that way. That he was born a freak and a monster. But that's not true. He's a monster because he made monstrous choices. Period. And I guess that pretty much sums up why I reached out to you. I've been working my way back through primary sources to get back to . . . well, to get back to the truth."

I'd gone into the conversation looking for any excuse to dismiss Greg's project and turn down his request to view my copy of the IHS. But instead I found myself wanting to help him. Greg was asking the same questions I'd been chasing my entire career. He wanted to know how a serial killer's mind works, what causes someone to kill, and what separates those individuals from everyone else. More important, he wasn't looking for an easy answer or quick fix. He valued the truth. And although I could tell there was something he'd left unsaid—something in the way he hesitated and pulled back toward the end of our conversation—I'd heard enough to agree to show him the cassette next time he was on the east coast.

———

That's how my connection with Greg began. He flew to Boston, I showed him the tape, we said we'd stay in touch. And from then on, he'd sporadically call or email me along the lines of: "I'm about to leave Montana after going to Kemper's childhood home. The dark basement where his mother sent him to sleep almost demands fantasies as a coping mechanism." Or "I found out that in the weeks prior to his mother's murder Kemper was living with a friend. I looked into him, and it turns out he was a violent sexual offender who apparently also had an extremely abusive mother."

Greg's enthusiasm made each sentence read like it ended with an exclamation mark. I admired his approach and was happy to share whatever insights I could from my days working alongside the agents of the BSU. But what surprised me was how relevant these conversations felt to the work I was doing now as an expert witness. It was odd. Because although Kemper had been an important resource during my days at the BSU—I'd leaned heavily on his prison interviews as I reimagined how the FBI studies, profiles, and catches serial killers—I'd never considered him beyond that narrow band of experience. Talking with Greg made me realize I'd missed an opportunity, that there was more to draw from the well. Kemper's insights on his crimes had been invaluable for my work at the BSU. I couldn't help but wonder what insights he had on his trial experience, and how that perspective might impact my work as an expert witness.

Then January 2020 rolled around. I opened my laptop to find a bunch of resolution-themed junk mail and a new email from

Greg. I read it once, then read it again: A belated Happy New Year. I hope you had a good holiday. I finally met with Kemper this weekend. A few things came up in my conversation with him that I'm hoping you might have insight on. Do you have time for a call?

It took me a moment to fully register those few brief sentences.

Kemper didn't accept visitors. He hadn't for more than twenty years—no visitors, no media requests, nothing beyond an occasional thank-you note to fans who sent him money or a letter of support. He wasn't even interested in parole. In fact, according to a lawyer who'd attended his hearing in 2007, Kemper considered himself unfit for society and preferred to spend the remainder of his days in prison, where he believed he belonged: "His feeling is that—and this is his belief—no one's ever going to let him out, and he's just happy, he's just happy going about his life in prison."

So why was he talking to Greg? And why now?

I typed out a response full of questions, then thought better and held down delete until my screen glowed anodyne white. I remembered Greg's evasiveness during our first call. How he hesitated when he talked about working back to primary sources. *This was why.* This meeting with Kemper must have been his goal all along. I don't know how he'd managed it, but the implications were profound—for law enforcement, for active cases, for victimology, and for probably even a whole lot more. Kemper could articulate with the sharpest detail all the thoughts, memories, and fantasies that swirled within his head. His mind was a rare asset.

Yes, I typed. Let me know what works for you.

I can't share the exact details of how Greg ended up speaking with Kemper—it involves people whose privacy he promised to respect. But I *can* answer the question of "Why Greg?"

It was because of Greg's commitment to the truth.

Kemper, as Greg explained it, had gotten tired of people making money off his crimes. Especially when their approach was so blatantly reductive, relying on sensationalism or tabloidesque headlines like "The Ogre of Aptos." Greg wrote: "He's particular about things being characterized accurately. In the middle of a cordial conversation, if I misquote a small detail like the time of day of one of his murders, or his height when he was arrested as a teenager, he's immediately annoyed and corrects me. So when others say or publish things about him that are wrong (some of his parole transcripts log him as 'Edmond' or 'Edward,' and even Douglas wrote about him having two younger sisters rather than one older and one younger), he sees it as a mischaracterization. That's why he shut himself off—he gave up on trusting anyone to get his story right."

This made sense to me. I'd applied the same rationale to the design of agent-offender interviews during my time at the FBI—the psychological trust building of "no one's ever understood you, but I do, and I want to help." What was interesting, though, was that Greg's approach wasn't artificial. See, there's a process that happens when you make an honest attempt at getting to know another person. It involves lowering your guard and opening yourself to the particular truths of how that person experiences the world. It's not easy, and there's no guarantee you'll like what you find, but it's vital. And if you're honest in your approach, if you communicate your respect to someone with clear intent, they sometimes give up their secrets. They show you their vulnerability and pride. Greg's commitment to hearing Kemper's particular truths stood in stark contrast to the entertainment-driven approach of countless storytellers who'd been corrupting the story for years.

The two had a second meeting, then a third, then routine meetings after that. We kept up our dialogue as well—me and Greg—mostly when Greg wanted to confirm certain facts or discuss aspects of Kemper's psychological makeup. The updates were fascinating and far more comprehensive than anything from my time at the FBI. They were different in key ways, too. Back then, Kemper's manner had been thinly veiled artifice. He liked the attention of the FBI, and he rose to meet the agents on equal footing. With Greg, Kemper seemed more open. More driven by the facts.

"Would you say he's being honest?" Greg asked.

"It's not an issue of honesty," I said. "You're asking for his story, and that's what you're getting. But it's *his* story—*his* version of the truth. And that's an important distinction because his truth is tied to an inherent disregard for humanity. You have to think about it that way, clinically almost, like he's giving you a diseased interpretation of events."

That was the one piece of unsolicited advice I gave. I didn't want to upset the dynamics that were already working for Greg in the first place.

It was during one of our next calls that I explained to Greg my interest in learning more about the offender side of the trial experience in connection to expert testimony.

"Kemper would be ideal for this," I said. "In large part because of how accountable and attentive he's always been. He's unique in that way. Most killers try to distance themselves from their actions by attributing them to 'the bad me,' or 'the other me,' or some other conveniently self-deceptive framework that absolves them from any emotional guilt. And eventually that just becomes part of their identity. I'm thinking of someone like Brian Dugan, who said *I wish I knew why I killed those girls. I wish I knew why I did a lot of things, but I don't.* Or Simonis, who said *I'd turn around and beat one, and then apologize for raping the other one. Sometimes I'd be nice and talk to them, but it's complex, there's so much involved that I don't understand. I don't know why I did certain things, why I raped some, why I beat some, why I burned some, and why I was nice to one but not another—I don't know. But I know it doesn't make sense."*

"Kemper certainly takes accountability," Greg said.

"Right. And it's partially a pride thing with him. But it's also important to know he had complete agency over his actions. I'm pretty sure he even talked about this in one of his interviews with Ressler."

"He definitely did," Greg confirmed. "He had a quote about wanting to bring his two worlds together: *the obscene, horrible, mass maniac world; and then the comfortable, normal, everybody-happy world. And I was bringing them together to where my reality made them compatible.* His words, not mine."

"That cuts to exactly the type of monomania I want to tap into—his monomania, not yours. You already said he's particular about small details and being characterized accurately. And I'm sure there were plenty of things that the psychiatrists and other experts got wrong during his trial. I bet that bothered him. And it might have even impacted the overall trial. Has he ever talked about any of this with you?"

"Not really," Greg said. "He tends to be fairly open and talkative about most things, but not so much with his trial. He's never said anything positive about the people involved in his case."

"Do you have a sense of why that is?"

"I think it goes back to that idea of being mischaracterized and feeling like he's being treated unfairly. Not that he's trying to deny his crimes or anything. But the whole arrest and trial was such a circus right from the start that I think it's only natural for him to lump in the trial experts with that same overall problem."

I sent Greg a list of questions to ask Kemper during his next visit to the prison in Vacaville, California, where Kemper was being held. But the approach didn't work. Their conversation lost its natural rhythm and became too stiff, too "interviewy." So Greg changed tack and went back to his original approach instead:

> **Horoupian:** What do you think about all the shit, though? When you see the stuff on . . . I'm trying to put myself in your shoes. If you're flipping the channels and you see your face at twenty-four with your mustache and cigarette hanging out of your mouth. Or you read something written about you. How do you think or feel or react to that?
>
> **Kemper:** Scary.
>
> **Horoupian:** Scary?
>
> **Kemper:** I know it won't be good. And sometimes, when it's bad, it's worse than bad because it's not true.

There was something about this exchange that made me dust off my old FBI-era cassettes. I wanted to listen to Kemper's early prison interviews with Douglas and Ressler. I wanted to hear his story in his own words. I'd never done that before—simply listen. I'd always filtered that experience through my own research or the needs of the BSU: pausing, taking notes, rewinding, listening sentence by sentence, pausing and rewinding again to pull out more data as I went.

But now, as I pushed aside my notebook and focused solely on the whirring cassette, I realized I'd missed something essential in how Kemper spoke. It was the way he homolyzed—the way he reconstructed each minute detail as something self-contained and perfectly whole. There was an element of world-building going on. Almost as if the particulars of language—its structure and integrity—functioned as a stitch that pulled together the fantasies in his head and the violence he'd enacted on reality itself. For Kemper, I realized, the details were more than just "getting the story right." They were sacrosanct. He saw killing as an act of ceremony. The purity of the details was his form of prayer.

"Sorry about that," Greg apologized to me during our next call. "The question-by-question approach hardly ever works. He bristles at interview mode and basically shuts off when I say something like *Tell me about your second coed victim* or *Tell me about your childhood in Montana.*"

"Good to know," I said. "Some of what worked for the agents was probably because of their authority dynamic and the thrill Kemper got from going toe-to-toe with them."

"I guess I don't have that level of cachet," Greg joked.

"So, how do you get him to open up when he doesn't want to talk about something?"

"It's a lot of following his lead and talking about the things he wants to talk about. I'll also bring in items connected to his personal life—like yearbook photos, for example—and that tends to be a good way of getting him to think about a time period or specific event I want him to talk about. It's those indirect approaches that work best."

These conversations with Greg were all taking place during the fall of 2022. As it so happened, it was just after the news broke of the University of Idaho student killings. The case, which was still unsolved at the time, was a major topic of conversation. I had no idea if Kemper was watching the news or paying attention, but it seemed like the type of thing a prison inmate must have at least heard about. I wondered if the case could be a way of getting him to open up. Maybe he'd make connections between his experiences and how things were playing out for this unknown killer in the media and by talking head experts.

It was worth a shot.

So I reached out to Greg, and we came up with a strategy for how he could mention this during his next trip to the prison. I sent him all the details of the crime I could find, as well as a breakdown of the victimology and several photos showing the victims and the location of the crime scene. Greg also read up on the case so he could be prepared for any questions Kemper might ask—"I picked up that technique from reading how the agents were always prepared to call out any lies that an offender might throw their way," Greg said.

Sadly, Kemper didn't have much to offer in return.

"I brought in the ten photos and placed them off to the side next to my water bottle and the ten individual sheets of paper I'm allowed to bring in. I didn't say anything about them. I just had them off to the side while we were talking. And after a few

minutes, he noticed and asked what they were about. He was acting sort of suspicious about them, so I said I'd tell him about them
later. I didn't mention them again until about two hours later.
Then I explained what I knew about the case—he said he hadn't
heard about it—and let him leaf through the photos. I emailed
you a few notes I wrote down."

I checked my computer to read through the notes while Greg
continued to talk:

> His first question was about whose cars were those parked
> outside.
>
> He said the house where the crimes took place was "weird
> looking."
>
> The skinned dog corpse found nearby might not have been
> because of the murderer; it could've been done by "a wannabe."
>
> If law enforcement had tried to speak to Ed through the
> media, he wouldn't have responded. He said, "Any evidence is
> evidence. And if you have no choice but to leave evidence dur-
> ing the crime, you don't wanna add to it."
>
> We talked about a footprint he had once left in mud with his
> size fifteen boot and how he decided not to create more foot-
> prints by climbing back down the embankment to try to erase it.
>
> He said he wished he had more to contribute, but there was
> nothing he saw in the photos or in the details I gave him.

"That was pretty much it," Greg said. "I asked about the media
coverage, too, but he said he typically only watches the news from
the local Sacramento channel, and that he doesn't follow any true
crime cases anyway. Not sure if that's useful or not."

"His comment about footprints is interesting," I said. "And also that his first question was about the cars. The agents zeroed in on cars right off the bat, too. They'd even do this thing where they'd profile the type of car a nonoffender was driving. So, like, if a journalist came to Quantico to interview the team, the agents would all write down a description of the car while someone was escorting the journalist back to the lot, then they'd see who was right in terms of make, model, color, year, etc. So the car thing is noteworthy, too. Maybe not useful, but noteworthy."

In the weeks that followed, I focused less on Kemper and more on my case work and the administrative side of getting ready for the classes I'd be teaching that spring. That's just the nature of research—you get an idea, you test it, and sometimes it doesn't pan out. Maybe Kemper's value was limited to crime scenes and didn't extend to the courtroom like I'd hoped. Maybe that well had run dry.

I'd accepted this as fact and was ready to move on when a long email came in from Greg with a subject line of "cars:"

"I was thinking about what you said about the agents profiling journalists' cars," Greg wrote.

I'm not sure if you know this, but Kemper stole a car as a teenager. The only written record of it is in his 1988 parole hearing transcript, where he mentions it very offhandedly. But to me it seems like a pretty big deal because he wasn't doing burglaries at that point in his life, and stealing a car is a pretty serious crime. And so I asked him about that, and he gave me a version of what happened that didn't really make sense.

Then, I started chipping away at all the details—this was over several months where I was pulling newspaper articles and was looking back through my notes from the trip I'd made to where this all happened in Helena, Montana—and what I found was that his story was about 90% of the truth and about 10% lies. Basically, if you look at a street map of Helena, there was no way he would have happened to end up where the car was stolen if he'd really been walking directly from the movie theater to his friend's house like he said he did.

So, I went back to him—not confrontational or like "you lied about this"—and I eased into talking about the car theft again. And then I said: "Were you just walking or were you futzing around doing other stuff?" And he paused and said: "Futzing around." And I said: "Okay, well, what do you mean?" And that's when he opened up. He knew that I'd done the leg work and I'd figured out the real story at that point, so he opened up and corrected that 10% he'd been lying about and explained that he and the guys he was with that night were breaking into cars looking for stuff in the glove box, and that they found keys in this specific car's glove box and decided to take it.

It was interesting enough that Greg had figured out a way of getting Kemper to drop his guard. That he'd learned from the agents and their approach of loading up on as much case information as possible, and he'd managed to adapt this to his own dynamics with Kemper, which were much more deferential and wait-a-minute-let-me-get-this-straight rather than the agents' combative back-and-forth. But what was even more interesting was that Greg had found the reason for *why* Kemper had lied about that 10 percent. He'd done the legwork and dug deeper into the case so that he could understand why someone so obsessed with the truth—remember, Kemper had turned his back on the world because of constant mischaracterizations—had been deceptive about this particular story. What made *this* event in particular so significant?

The answer had to do with family and the solipsistic way in which Kemper responded to the emotions of his past. If you look in the morning paper of that same Friday, the one Kemper spent breaking into cars, you'll find a divorce announcement. The announcement names Kemper's mom and her second husband—Kemper's first stepfather—Norman, whom Kemper admired and looked up to in the absence of his own dad. With Norman gone, there was no more father figure at home. There was no buffer. It was just Kemper and his mom, the woman he blamed for all his problems. Divorce was the stressor. It triggered him to lash out. By holding that detail back, Kemper was showing how significant and personal the divorce truly was.

"Did you mention any of this the next time you saw him?" I asked.

"Yeah. He gave me a typical shrug. He has this shrug he does that's essentially, *I got nothing more to add.* It's basically like, *Yeah, makes sense, good work.*"

There was no grand revelation here. No paradigm-shifting truth. I'd hoped that Kemper would teach me something new about working with offenders as part of the trial process, but he simply reinforced the importance of loading up on the facts, building trust, and creating accountability.

Still, it was validating to hear that this authentic approach actually worked.

So much of the trial process is pageantry. It's gamesmanship and half-truths and lawyers using confirmation bias to build out structurally sound but deceptive cases. In a lot of ways, it speaks to the binary nature of the trial process. There's not a whole lot of space for the complexities of the human experience when you're tasked with filtering someone's actions down to good or bad, guilty or not guilty, right or wrong. But as Greg saw with Kemper, this type of thinking only perpetuates myths and absolves criminals of their accountability. It doesn't get to the root of those problems. It doesn't get people to think in different ways about those myths and our culture at large.

I don't have a solution, but I hope my experience can serve as a building block for someone else who can take this further.

Sometimes you answer the big questions, and sometimes the best you can hope for is to make the path easier for the next person who comes along to figure it out.

CHAPTER 10

Victim Impact Statements

The report was one of the worst I'd ever seen. It confirmed decades of rumors, validating countless whispers of a monster on campus, a predator who ruined life after life, year after year, unaccountable and unchallenged despite credible evidence of the abhorrent events taking place behind his training room door.

"You're not alone," one victim told another.

"You don't have to worry," another murmured reassuringly. "He does that to me all the time, too."

They'd try to normalize their experiences, comforting each other, because what more could they do? After all, there had already been several documented attempts early on where young women had confided the horrors they'd experienced to their coaches and counselors in hopes they might be heard—and still, no one took action. At best, those in a position to do something simply turned a blind eye. At worst, they suggested that the accusers themselves were somehow "mistaken."

And so it was that from 1994 to 2016, while employed as a

doctor for Michigan State University, the United States national gymnastics team, and at several elite private gyms around the country, Larry Nassar was able to harass, abuse, and perform sexually intrusive examinations on more than five hundred known victims.

The scope of the case was enormous. Even today, it stands as one of the largest examples of sexual exploitation by a single person in U.S. history. What makes it even worse is that it was perpetrated by a man who was *supposed* to be the safety net for the vulnerable—a physician who was there to *protect* his patients.

More than five hundred victims. It's easy to get caught up in the numbers alone, especially at this kind of magnitude, but it's important to remember that there were five hundred individual victims—five hundred young women and girls—whose lives were forever changed for the worse by Larry Nassar.

I got involved in the Nassar case starting in the spring of 2018, in the immediate aftermath of a series of damning accusations levied against Nassar by several former USA Gymnastics medalists and team members. As is often the case, it was this sway of prominent names that caused the media (and the public at large) to start paying attention.

Then the floodgates opened.

More women came forward. And then even more. Their bravery empowered one another, launching one wave after the next. The sheer volume of victims—150 when I started, and more and more coming forward each day—necessitated a concomitant number of subject matter experts to contribute their insights to the case as well. Each and every single victim needed to be interviewed and assessed. Their stories and experiences needed to be catalogued, analyzed, and made measurable in the form of both an evaluative report and a victim impact statement. This necessary part of the judicial process allowed each victim the right to stand up in court and deliver their own *individual* account of the trauma Nassar had caused them. Since the goal of this process was to personalize each victim's experience while maintaining the standards of evidence-based trauma assessment, and since I'd developed a reputation for doing this exact type of work on similarly high-profile cases throughout my career, the prosecution reached out to me to see if I could help with the assessment of one victim in particular.

My initial contact with a young woman I'll refer to as M. was via the phone, which wasn't exactly ideal. I've always preferred face-to-face interactions so I can see the person I'm working with; it really helps me to observe the subtle interplay between their spoken words and their corresponding physical responses. Plus, I want these individuals I'm observing to see *me* as well—because that's how trauma-informed interviewing works best. It's about empathy and understanding and establishing trust. And that's a lot easier to do—*and* more effective—when you're sharing the same physical space with another person.

Though the numbers would help bolster the victims' case against Nassar, I knew it could also become an issue in my interview with M., and I was eager to get out ahead of it. I didn't want her feeling like just another data point or box to be checked. I wanted her to feel seen, heard, acknowledged. And more than anything, I genuinely wanted to help her learn how to integrate this experience into her life so that she could continue to heal and move forward.

Knowing the phone posed a barrier right from the outset, I scheduled a longer-than-normal initial interview so I could focus on building up a connection with M. first. I started off by asking about her upbringing, her interests, and how she spent her free time. I then followed up with another question whenever she was engaged positively, and I steered the conversation away from topics that seemed to trigger emotionally intense responses. Essentially, I was laying the groundwork for the tough topics still to come. And when M. was ready, when our conversation became less stilted and a little more even in its back-and-forth, I broached the topic of how she'd first met Nassar.

"It was early on," she recalled. "I'd developed a pretty bad injury that prevented me from competing. I was working with my own trainer at first. But the injury wasn't getting better, so the coaches suggested I see Dr. Nassar."

"Did you know anything about him at the time?" I inquired.

"Not really. I'd seen him interacting with other athletes. But he only worked with people whose injuries kept them from competing. None of my friends knew Nassar personally, either. They all just repeated what everyone else said, that he was one of the best at what he did."

"And what were your first impressions of him?"

"I remember thinking he was nerdy," she said. "A small, friendly guy who wore glasses and laughed and would pat other athletes on their back. Kind of goofy. But at the same time, there was still something impressive about him, because he'd worked with some of the best Olympic athletes. I don't know if that makes sense or not. But I remember that being part of why I trusted him when he told me that his treatments weren't conventional, but that they worked."

"Do you want to talk about those treatment sessions?" I asked.

M. paused. "I'm super embarrassed and feel like a fool that I used to think it was medical," she admitted, letting the words sink in. "And I'm not sure I ever even *did* think it was a medical treatment. But that's how I buried it. That's how I dealt with it whenever it popped into my head. I just told myself it was really weird, but what did I know?"

The first time she realized something was wrong, M. found herself in a long room with Nassar at MSU's Sports Medicine center. She remembered the door being open at the end; she could hear other people walking just outside, back and forth. Nassar instructed M. to lie down on a table so he could perform a type of stretching therapy. Then, without warning or explanation, he inserted his fingers inside her vagina, applied pressure, and pushed inside toward her leg. M. thought he was trying to get to the hamstrings. She described being instantly aware that something about this "treatment" was off, but then again, she knew that part of being an athlete was learning how to mentally ignore pain along with any intrusive thoughts that might get in the way of her athletic goals. Her feelings of pride confused the matter even further.

"I was so thrilled to be a scholarship athlete at MSU. I was living out a dream," she explained to me. "I didn't want to do anything that might compromise eighteen years of hard work and sacrifice. Besides, the whole thing only lasted a few minutes, anyways."

Nassar performed the same treatment on M. a total of three times. He scheduled her for a fourth session, but during that final treatment, M. noticed that he was keeping his eyes closed and that he had an erection. That was the final straw. She ran out of the room and never went back. Then she buried the memory deep down for the next twenty years.

I could tell that it wasn't easy for M. to talk about her experiences. Years of calcified, unprocessed, and untreated trauma is a heavy burden for a person to carry under *any* circumstances. But I think what made the whole thing even worse for M. was that she'd tried to talk about it once before. She'd taken the risk of lowering her guard and telling her story to an investigator for MSU right after that third "treatment," but her claims had been dismissed. The investigator she spoke with waved off her complaint, informing her that she was "overreacting" to a common treatment known as pelvic floor therapy. That invalidating interaction brought back the flood of shame and embarrassment all over again. In an act of self-protection, M. raised up her guard and promised to seal off the memories for good—until recently.

"What changed?" I asked, curious.

"I guess it was seeing all the accusations coming out on the news," M. replied. "I started getting flashbacks of my treatment sessions with Nassar. Like, I'd be standing in the grocery store and see someone who looked like Nassar and start getting these flashbacks. I couldn't control them. I was feeling anxious all the time, too. That's when I knew I had to come forward."

Flashbacks are a common symptom of trauma. They transport

the victim back to the moment of trauma itself—emotionally, psychologically, and sensorily. They occur unexpectedly and tend to be extremely vivid, upsetting, and disruptive to daily life. They're also intensely disorienting in how they hijack the brain and affectively replace the present with the past, not unlike a scratched record looping the same fractured moment over and over again. I explained all of this to M., assuring her that her experiences were totally normal. Then I suggested that if she wanted to better understand and process her trauma, it might be a good idea to start with a self-survey report.

"It basically personalizes the nature of your experiences," I clarified. "It's *your* record of what happened. It's a tool for describing your specific psychological aftereffects, their severity, and how they developed as a result of your victimization."

M. was interested in two of the surveys I'd mentioned—an Impact of Event survey and the Beck Depression Index—both of which are highly regarded across medical and judicial institutions. I administered these as part of our phone interviews and included the results in my assessment report, which is summarized below. It starts with my opinion and works backward to show the rationale that informed these professional beliefs.

Opinion

After interviewing and testing M. and reading the media accounts regarding Larry Nassar, it is my opinion that she is suffering from symptoms of a delayed post-traumatic stress response to her victimization by Larry Nassar at age 18. I base my opinions on my education, background, training, research, and clinical practice with hundreds of victims of crimes. My opinions are rendered within a reasonable degree of medical and psychological probability.

Background

M. was born in the Northeast, had a typical childhood, did well in school, and was a nationally ranked athlete in high school. Her coach encouraged her to pursue her athletic potential and taught her to be mentally strong and to never "be the victim of anything."

While she was in high school, M. was recruited by Michigan State University and offered an athletic scholarship of $40,000/year. It was a dream come true, and she accepted.

M. thrived at MSU as an athlete and within her academic courses. But her constant training led to a debilitating injury that required surgery. Her recovery was slow and full of setbacks from chronic, radiating pain. This led to her meetings with Nassar.

Delayed Disclosure

M. described feeling "like a nerve shot through me" when the news of Nassar's abuse first broke. She'd spent decades burying her memories. She'd never told her mother, her friends, or her husband. She thought about finally opening up. But she was nervous. And as more women came forward, M. was shocked to hear critics blaming the women for not coming forward earlier rather than supporting them. She didn't want to experience that same reaction. She had a wonderful husband and children and was afraid of doing anything to disrupt her life with them. She just wanted to be left alone. So when people who knew about her athletic days at MSU started asking if she knew him, she was quick to say no. She already felt enough shame and embarrassment and didn't want to exacerbate this by being in the public eye.

Beck Depression Index

M.'s results indicate that she has a borderline clinical depression (n=19). Symptoms indicating distress are as follows: She feels sad and that she has failed more than the average person. She doesn't enjoy things as she once did, feels guilty a good part of the time, and feels she may be punished. She is disappointed in and feels critical of herself. She cries more than she used to, feels irritated all the time, feels indecisive, takes extra effort to get started at something, doesn't sleep as well, tires easily, stomach is acidic, worries about physical problems like upset stomach, and is less interested in sex than she used to be.

Impact of Event Scale

The results here show that M. is clearly suffering many symptoms (total score of 65). She is high on intrusive thoughts (n=29), moderate on avoidant strategies (n=22), and moderate on hyperarousal symptoms (n=14). These scores indicate that she has repeated intrusive thoughts and reminders of the medical abuse and is unable to avoid thinking about it. Reminders bring back feelings about it at least once/week. Other things make her think about it, and she had strong waves of feelings about it. She tries to avoid letting herself get upset when thinking of it, tries to remove it from memory, has dreams about it, and tries not to talk about it. On hyperarousal, she felt irritable and angry, had trouble concentrating.

Professional Analysis

This case is about two interconnected events spanning a long period of time: molestation during medical treatment and the psychological impact that occurred when memories of that molestation resurfaced in response to news coverage of the Nassar case and M.'s own delayed disclosure. The resulting impact is a clear case of trauma. M.'s symptoms include severe anxiety and flashbacks, disturbed sleep, strained relationships, and feelings of guilt about not speaking up at the time of the abuse or taking other steps to stop it. She expressed feeling "super embarrassed" about letting Nassar do this to her. She also described how the experience haunts her and that she can't get Nassar out of her head during certain personal and private moments.

Currently, and especially given the fact that M. hasn't yet had the benefit of professional counseling, I see M. as having a distinct risk of becoming emotionally overwhelmed and depressed. It is my strong recommendation that she starts counseling with a trauma therapist and that she be evaluated for Eye Movement Desensitization and Reprocessing therapy—a structured psychotherapy treatment designed to alleviate the distress associated with traumatic memories. I also recommend couples therapy to help navigate the current vulnerabilities in her relationship, and an advanced program in martial arts.

It is critical that these traumatic issues be addressed in order that M.'s future ability to feel secure in the world and to trust others improves. At best, I believe the post-trauma memories are permanent, but over time can be treated as describe above.

———

I never spoke with M. again. My job in this case was to evaluate the severity of her trauma, write up an official report, and move on. But I was never good at simply moving on from people who'd opened up to me and given me their trust. I thought about M. often throughout the weeks and months as the Nassar case continued to dominate the news cycle and inspire a cultural reckoning, with new revelations spilling out on what seemed like a near-daily basis. I was particularly disheartened—though not entirely shocked—to learn that the abuse had been reported to the university early on, but instead of taking action against Nassar (a celebrated doctor with a reputation that helped bolster that of the school), they'd instead used this information to prepare for an inevitable public relations crisis.

Of course, MSU initially denied these allegations. School officials pointed to an "independent review" that they'd conducted in 2014 after receiving a complaint about Nassar behaving inappropriately, and noted that its conclusion—which was largely based on consultation with Nassar's colleagues, mind you—indicated no wrongdoings "of a sexual nature." But this wasn't quite the full story. In fact, MSU's investigation, court records later showed, hadn't been independently conducted at all. No, it had been a privately conducted internal review, intended to shield the university from any potential liabilities. Even the head of the review team itself, former federal prosecutor Patrick J. Fitzgerald, acknowledged the confusion and implicit misrepresentation of his role in the case, stating: "We were engaged to provide counsel regarding anticipated litigation and to make sure that any internal reviews did not interfere with the two law enforcement inquiries underway."

This news was damning, to say the least. It spoke to a systematic failure that, in effect, cast MSU as a second offender in the case. Nassar may have committed the initial abuse, but it was the university's inaction—its complicit denial—that perpetuated the abuse and provoked further trauma that should have never occurred.

This was about so much more than the athletes who were hurt, or the man who hurt them.

This was about institutional betrayal at its *worst*.

It was validating to watch the media demand accountability as the case continued to play out. For once, the media followed the story and dedicated real resources to its coverage. Whereas, just several years prior, this level of attention for a case like this— one centering around the rights of the victims, as opposed to a perpetrator—would've been unimaginable. Now suddenly there were front-page articles, prime-time news, and a scrum of reporters from every major media outlet lining the walls of the Ingham

County Circuit Court in Lansing, Michigan, to capture every word of the trial.

But the part that impressed me most was the dignity that the victims were treated with, especially within the scope of the case. They were given a platform. They were allowed to speak. While the whole world was watching, Judge Rosemarie Aquilina allowed 156 women to step forward and share their own personal victim impact statement. This lasted for seven days and was broadcast on live TV. It was important for the public to hear, but its greater importance was for the individuals themselves, allowing each of them to retake control over their own story.

Not everyone saw the merits of Judge Aquilina's decision. Some called it theatrical. Some called it self-congratulatory. And there was one news article that questioned whether the whole thing was a throwback to the days of public hangings.

But all in all, the outcry was as predictable as it was reductive. I'd heard variations of this same thing throughout my entire career, and it always boiled down to the same thing: the fear of deviating from the status quo. For the judicial system—same as I'd seen within the similarly rigid systems of academia and the FBI—change was anathema. There was always an old guard that cared more about upholding tradition than making progress and adapting with the times. In this case, the old guard didn't approve of giving victims an opportunity to speak for the same reason they didn't approve of anything that added nuance to a trial. They wanted to keep everything as flat and straightforward as possible, reducing all its complicated variables down to a numbing sameness: the prosecution and defense; the victim and offender; the good guys, the bad guys, and the disinterested virtues of law itself.

But humanity itself isn't quite so cut-and-dried.

Over time, the details of even the most shocking cases tend to fade. This was true of the Nassar case as well. Nowadays, people remember the nature of the abuse, and they might even remember the central figures of Nassar and MSU and U.S. Gymnastics, but they forget the 156 victims who spoke out at trial and the countless others who remain voiceless. Instead, those individuals have all been condensed—with the exception of a media-selected few—into a singular blurred collective of sadness, outrage, and pain.

But their individual stories still matter. As one survivor shared with me:

The whole thing was a big circle of horribleness. It took me years to come forward and tell anyone. Even after the story finally broke and all these amazing gymnasts started coming forward, I had doubts. It was like, "What are my bosses going to think?" "What are my friends going to think?" "Will I have a target on the back?" "Will anyone even believe me?" But then, eventually, these questions felt less important and there was this other question that started cutting through all the fear, and I started thinking, "What if I can make a difference and change one person's life or get one other person like me to come forward?"

And so, I went public. I made the choice to do it and to not hold back. I talked about how I was abused starting when I was fifteen and continued for about five years during my time with USA Gymnastics. I talked about going to national team training camp nearly every month, and how those camps would last anywhere from like four to seven days each time. And I explained that I was just one of dozens of girls getting treatment about three times a day. So, you do the math. That's a lot of abuse that was happening, right? It adds up pretty quickly.

And the part about coming forward that really surprised me was that I got a lot of positive feedback, a lot of support. And part of that was other gymnasts privately messaging me and saying things like, *Thank you so much for coming out and telling your story. I had the same thing happen to me.* And one of those messages said, *You know, you may not remember me, but I looked up to you as a gymnast and we were at the same competition one year.* I was like, I think I got, like, last place in that competition. This other girl that messaged me, and she goes, *But I remember you walked out of the training room with Larry. I was walking in and he said, "I did a manipulation on your friend there and it worked. So I'll do it on you, too."* And because this girl looked up to me, she was like, "Whatever you did to her, she's the best, so do it to me because it's going to help my injuries, too."

And the point of all this is that it's so easy to manipulate people. And I think it's important to recognize that you never really know whose path you're crossing because there's this culture of fear and silence and manipulation that encourages people to suffer silently and blame themselves. And if you give into that cultural pressure to keep quiet, you might make things worse. But you don't have to. There's *always* a choice. You can choose to step forward and share your truth regardless of how difficult or overwhelming it might seem, you can break that circle of horribleness. That's something *you* get to choose.

Choice is something victims often feel that they've lost. When describing their experiences, they often use words like "helpless," "isolated," and "alone." It's a feeling that's rooted in their original trauma and continues through the investigative process and legal process as well. And that's exactly why individual stories matter so much. Cases like Nassar's, where so many victims came forward and shared their personal stories in their own unique voice—it flips the narrative on its head. Victims no longer feel isolated. They feel connected.

And this is what makes the victim impact statements so powerful. By choosing to come forward, they're giving other victims that choice, too—and an opportunity to take back control.

On the Horizon

I'll be honest. There have been a few times throughout my career when I've struggled to stay objective. It feels like a tug-of-war between my empathy for those involved and my professional responsibility to remain impartial. I would never deny this. I'm not a machine—not someone who can turn off compassion by simply flipping a switch. And while I sometimes wish it were that easy, I never lose sight of the fact that being an expert means working with real people on real cases where the outcomes really matter. The job's about more than just the evidence and facts; it's about the lives intertwined with them. And, yes, of course this work demands objectivity, but it also demands a level of humanity to keep connected to the importance of what I do, even when walking that fine line feels almost impossible.

I think about the Menendez case, for example, where I got to know Erik and Lyle. The complexity of their abuse was destructive and damaging. It was the stuff of nightmares. To experience such depths of physical and psychological abuse at the hands of their parents—that's a fate no child should suffer. And while I firmly believed they deserved to be held accountable for killing their mom and dad, I also believed they deserved some sort of clemency for the years of trauma that led up to the violence that occurred on the night of their parents' deaths.

The same holds true for Andrea Constand. She suffered deeply because of Bill Cosby's horrific actions. His barbarism corrupted not only her life but the lives of dozens of other women over a period of decades. And for what? For the fleeting pleasure of one man's sexual gratification? For ego? For a fantasy of dominance and control? And as if that weren't bad enough, he got away with it year after year because of wealth, power, and firmly entrenched bias against victims of sexual assault.

And then there are cases like Larry Nassar. Those cases—especially the ones involving children—are far and away the worst. They're a shock so visceral that I can't imagine feeling anything but sympathy for the victims. The actions of Nassar, the abuse he imposed on hundreds of young girls whose innocence and trust were violated in the most absolute sense of the word—were heartless. They made me sick.

So, yes, I have strong feelings about a lot of my cases. And I'll readily admit that. But I'm also aware of those feelings, and I take steps to carefully balance them with an equally strong respect for the integrity of my role as an expert witness. I don't pick sides. I don't indulge in any judgments. I simply present my expertise as accurately and clearly as I possibly can. And that holds true regardless of how much a case gnaws at my conscience or sparks frustration. My responsibility is to the process. And my objectivity is what gives my testimony its value.

This need for conviction in expert testimony is more important than ever. *Truth* is more important than ever, especially because courtrooms aren't always the stalwart institutions we'd like to believe they are. I saw bias slip into the Duke lacrosse case, where Durham County district attorney Mike Nifong attempted to politicize allegations of rape to fit his own personal agenda of gaining favor in a reelection year. And I saw a similar instance of bias when an Illinois state attorney, Jeffrey Tomczak, aggressively demanded the death penalty in what turned out to be a wrongful allegation case involving a fourteen-and-a-half-hour interrogation of a man named Kevin Fox, who was coerced by police into falsely confessing to the murder of his own three-year-old daughter. A subsequent report said that Tomczak appeared to exploit the case in a bid to win reelection in a tightly contested race.

Bias can be pervasive. Even a single lapse can erode an individual expert's credibility, which in turn destabilizes the trust placed in our profession as a whole. This is the inherent challenge of our work: to transcend personal beliefs, biases, and political influences to deliver the truth as it is—not as we might wish it to be. Impartiality isn't merely our obligation; it's the bedrock of justice itself. It's the promise on which the entire legal system relies.

In recent years, I've noticed that trust between juries and expert witnesses has started to grow thin again. It's part of a broader societal skepticism directed toward expertise as a whole. Where professional experts were once seen as impartial arbiters of truth, we're now questioned as to whether our testimony serves the facts or the party paying our fees. This uncertainty has been further exacerbated by high-profile cases where dueling experts hold starkly opposing beliefs, leaving juries to wonder if the title of "expert" is merely a tool for advocacy rather than a badge of neutrality.

The case of Sally Clark comes to mind when I think about this dichotomy between testimony and distrust. In 1999, Sally Clark, a solicitor and mother of two, was convicted in the UK for the murders of her infant sons, both of whom had suddenly died within months of each other. In building their argument, prosecutors relied heavily on the testimony of pediatrician Roy Meadow, who asserted that the likelihood of two sudden infant death syndrome (SIDS) events in a family like Clark's was 1 in 73 million, implying to the jury that this was an absurd statistical improbability. The problem with Meadow's testimony was that it introduced what's known as the prosecutor's fallacy—a logical error that occurs when someone mistakenly assumes that the probability of finding evidence against an innocent person is the same as the probability that a person is guilty. In Clark's case specifically, the calculation ignored genetic or environmental factors that could increase the likelihood of a second SIDS case. Meadow's flawed rationale should never have been allowed in court in the first place, and yet it had a huge impact on the jury's eventual decision.

The situation was compounded in the trial's aftermath, when forensic pathologist Alan Williams conducted postmortem examinations which revealed that one of the babies may have in fact died of an infection. The implications for Clark's innocence were huge. And yet, inexplicably, Williams did not submit his findings to the court. His rationale? "I just assumed they had already seen them and, as I had said, they were not of any relevance."

It wasn't until 2003 that Williams's findings were revealed and

Meadow's statistical fallacy came to light. Clark had spent more than three years in prison by the time her conviction was finally overturned. Her nightmare experience underscores the need for accuracy in expert testimony, proper understanding of probabilities in legal contexts, and safeguards against confirmation bias. Sadly, the wrongful conviction and the loss of her sons exacted a profound toll on Sally Clark, who passed away in 2007, a victim of systemic failure and public misunderstanding.

Though tragic, faulty testimony does occur. Usually it's avoidable, sometimes it's not. But it only tells part of the story of growing mistrust between juries and expert witnesses. The other key factor has to do with the rise of what's known as "the armchair expert."

The phenomenon of the armchair expert grew from the digital age, where access to vast reservoirs of information has empowered individuals to speak authoritatively on wide-ranging topics. Social media platforms and online forums amplify these voices, blurring the lines between expertise and opinion. What once required years of study and practice can now, at least superficially, be replaced by a quick internet search and the whims of personalized recommendation algorithms. This democratization of knowledge has its merits, to be sure. There are plenty of examples of armchair experts solving crimes, rewriting past injustices, or creating novel solutions to previously unsolvable problems.

But problems arise when, with so much information—accurate or otherwise—at the world's fingertips, people start to form strong opinions on complex topics without the depth of understanding that years of study and experience provide. In the courtroom, this dynamic can manifest as skepticism or outright distrust toward expert witnesses, whose carefully researched testimony may clash with the assumptions jurors have already formed. This widening gap has made it increasingly difficult for experts to bridge the divide, requiring them to go beyond simply conveying their findings, but doing so in a way that reestablishes the value of authentic expertise in an age where everyone with an internet connection believes they have all the answers.

I don't make this observation to be dismissive. If anything, I'm impressed by the modern-day alchemy of it all—the way in which technology continuously redefines the boundaries of what is possible. And I'm fully convinced that expert witnesses need to start adapting to the rapid pace of change if our profession is to stay relevant. Artificial intelligence, in particular, has huge potential to overhaul the utility of expert witnesses in the courtroom, because it allows for inarguable fact to come to the forefront without the risk of being tainted by human error or subjectivity. The applications are profound.

Back in the late 1980s, I saw AI as the next logical step in the future of computing. The technology was still a ways off, I knew, but the practical applications made it all but inevitable. So I wrote a grant proposal to get ahead of the game and see what was possible. My idea was to use AI to speed up data analysis. The concept was rooted in my ongoing work to develop behavioral profiling for the FBI—a time-consuming task of sorting through interviews of convicted serial killer cases to learn about the patterns and motivations of their crimes so as to understand the specific psychological compositions of their minds. At one point, I realized that this exact process could be sped up dramatically using an AI tool called a large language model (LLM)—basically a system for using deep-learning techniques and massively large data sets to understand and summarize human language by processing vast amounts of text data. In other words, if my grant went through, I could use an LLM to process interviews with hundreds of offenders from all around the country in seconds. And I could repeat the process for different types of offenders, too.

Of course, this big idea hinged on the ever-uncertain variable of receiving funding first. And that's always a roll of the dice. So I wasn't exactly surprised when my $60,000 proposal was rejected by my unit chief at the FBI. I can't remember the exact phrasing of his letter—I was quick to stuff it into the trash—but it was something along the lines of "These types of grants are intended for scientific research, not science fiction." And so my early aspirations of AI were put on hold. I'd have to wait several decades for the capabilities of computers to catch up to the designs I'd mapped out in my head.

Fast-forward to the spring of 2024. It's still nascent, but AI is now weaving its way through our day-to-day existence in the form of chatbots, search engines, digital assistants, and content generators for voice, image, and video. I've started seeing AI trickle into the legal system, too. A simple example is the use of AI to sift through massive amounts of data to quickly and accurately spot patterns and connections that might be missed otherwise. I'm also in touch with public defenders who are tapping into the potential of AI as a means of drafting legal documents and conducting basic research.

A more novel example is the use of AI to virtually re-create crimes or disputed scenarios. Through this innovative approach, juries can immerse themselves in the specific details of the events in question, gaining a vivid and precise understanding of what transpired. These simulations are not stand-alone; they are guided by expert witnesses who provide crucial context and objective commentary in a way that makes sense to a judge and jury. This collaborative synergy between technology and human expertise underscores the true potential of AI—not as a replacement for professional insight, but as a tool to augment it. By empowering expert witnesses with enhanced clarity and precision, this partnership fosters more informed deliberations and promotes fairer outcomes in the pursuit of justice.

All of these single tools and use cases for AI are certainly worth exploring on their own. But I think the next step in AI's evolution is where we'll really see a paradigm-shifting impact. For me, that means looking at the big picture of integrating disparate AI tools to create a novel ecosystem capable of solving large-scale problems. In other words, I'm trying to bridge law enforcement to the judicial system so that AI works seamlessly across all stages—prevention, investigation, legal proceedings, and rehabilitation—to create a more efficient, responsive, and predictive criminal justice system.

Currently, the work I'm doing uses natural language processing techniques to analyze the manifestos of lone offenders and improve how we assess potential threats. The goal is to uncover hidden patterns and themes in written texts, allowing for a more thorough understanding of what might indicate a risk of violence.

The analysis looks for both clear and subtle signs of violence, personal grievances, and specific ideologies, focusing on topics like race, societal issues, and existential beliefs. It uses hierarchical clustering and similarity measures to show how closely related certain topics are. For example, the study identifies common themes of hate, violence, societal frustration, and emotional distress. By focusing on themes rather than individual words, I'm able to see the bigger picture, uncovering deeper patterns that might indicate a threat, and how urgently a threat needs to be investigated.

One key benefit of using machine learning for this type of analysis is its ability to quickly process large amounts of data, especially from platforms like Reddit, 4chan, and Telegram, where lone offenders often share their manifestos. The limit is that, while machine learning excels at identifying patterns in text, human judgment is still better at making the final call on threat assessment. This hybrid approach helps ensure that machine learning supports, rather than replaces, human decision-making. It's a means of proactively mitigating risks by analyzing pre-offense writings and enhancing the objectivity and efficiency of threat evaluation.

The next step will be to apply this same methodology to risk assessment for sentencing and parole decisions. All it takes is building out a database of past cases and court transcripts. In doing so, machine learning can be used to evaluate the likelihood of re-offending when making decisions about sentencing, bail, or parole. At the same time, this analysis can account for bias in terms of racial, socioeconomic, or gender-based disparities in arrests, sentencing, or parole decisions, ensuring greater fairness within judicial processes.

I'm fully aware how dystopian this sounds—my students and colleagues never hesitate to remind me. And I get it. But I've never been much of a fatalist. Instead, I believe we get to shape what type of world we live in. This stems from my early days working with victims of trauma and rape back in the 1970s. For a lot of those women, it would have been easy to feel defeated. But they refused to accept that as their fate. Women in the early '70s *pushed back*. They challenged societal constraints to reimagine a world that better accounted for their role within it. And, consequently, their resilience and determination became a powerful testament to the transformative potential of collective action.

In the 1980s, I witnessed another cultural shift take place in terms of mental health. Advocacy groups gained prominence and began demanding better treatment options, policy reform, and the destigmatization of mental illness, elevating the importance of mental health care as a public health priority. Similarly, the '90s faced issues of globalization, the dot-com era, and the culture wars of identity politics. The 2000s saw issues of climate change, the great recession, and the rise of social media.

On and on, each decade has faced its own anxieties, innovations, and disruptions. And in every era, there are those who stand at the crossroads of chaos and clarity, tasked with illuminating the path forward. The role of the expert witness is not simply to testify to facts, but to serve as a beacon of truth in times of uncertainty. It is a calling to navigate the fractures of the present with wisdom and to lend meaning to the questions that define an evolving world.

To bear witness in such a capacity is to stand in the currents of change, where the familiar unravels and the future is contested. The expert witness is both participant and observer, a voice that steadies the tumult while never shying away from its complexities. In this role, truth is not a static endpoint but a living force—one that seeks to heal, to reconcile, and to inspire.

Ours is an age of extraordinary transformation, shaped by the promise and peril of new frontiers. From the surge of artificial intelligence to the reimagining of cultural norms, the contours of society are shifting in profound and often disorienting ways. Yet, as in every age of disruption, there remains an enduring principle: The future is not given; it is forged. And it is in this forging that the expert witness finds their purpose—not as a passive observer, but as a steward of integrity, clarity, and justice.

The work is not easy. It demands courage to confront entrenched biases, to question the narratives of power, and to stand firm in the face of doubt. It asks for humility, an openness to complexity, and an unwavering commitment to fairness. To be an expert witness is to embrace the tension between knowledge and empathy, precision and humanity. It is to see the thread of shared experience that binds us, even in moments of fracture, and to weave that thread into something stronger.

And yet, there is beauty in this labor. In every truth spoken, a new possibility emerges. In every injustice challenged, a new foundation is laid. The expert witness, in their quiet resolve, transforms the raw material of discord into something enduring—into understanding, into unity, into hope.

In times of great change, the expert witness becomes more than a figure of expertise. They become a keeper of values, of justice, and a reminder that even amid disruption, we have the power to help shape what comes next.

To serve as an expert witness is to stand in the stream of history and declare that truth *matters*. It is to light the way forward—not just for those around us, but for the generations who will follow.

Acknowledgments

We owe a great deal of thanks to the many individuals who have helped shape this book along the way.

To our agent, Alice Martell, who is a great advocate and friend.

To our editor, Carrie Napolitano, who has been a constant source of inspiration and encouragement. To our bonus editor, Ian Dorset, who is the rare type who can fill big shoes. And to everyone else at Grand Central Publishing who has helped see this project to completion.

Bibliography

Burgess, Ann Wolbert, and Lynda Lytle Holmstrom. "Rape Trauma Syndrome," *American Journal of Psychiatry* 131 (1974): 981–986.

Burgess, Ann Wolbert, and Lynda Lytle Holmstrom. "The Rape Victim in the Emergency Ward," *American Journal of Nursing* 73 (October 1973): 1741–1745.

Constand, A. *The Moment: Standing Up to Bill Cosby, Speaking Up for Women* (New York: Viking, 2021).

Douglas, J. E., A. W. Burgess, and R. K. Ressler. *Sexual Homicide: Patterns and Motives* (New York: Free Press, 1988).

Lanning, K. *Love, Bombs, and Molesters: An FBI Agent's Journey* (self published, 2018).

Ressler, R. K., J. E. Douglas, A. W. Burgess, and A. G. Burgess. *Crime Classification Manual: A Standard System for Investigating and Classifying Violent Crime*, 3rd ed. (New York: Wiley, 2013).

Ressler, Robert K., and Tom Shachtman. *Whoever Fights Monsters: My Twenty Years Tracking Serial Killers for the FBI* (New York: St. Martins, 1993).

Stone, M. H. and G. Brucato. *The New Evil: Understanding the Emergence of Modern Violent Crime* (Amherst, NY: Prometheus, 2019).

Index

Beck, Aaron T., 158
Beck Depression Index, 158, 197, 199
behavioral profiling, 212–213
Behavioral Science Unit (BSU), FBI's,
    63, 64, 94, 122, 175, 176, 178, 184
Bendectin, 16
bias
  AI data analysis and, 215
  confirmation, 86, 176, 190, 211
  confronting, 217
  Duke University lacrosse team
    case and, 120–121
  of family and friends, 156
  within judicial system, 209
  against victims, 208
bipolar disorder, 119
blood pressure test, 13–14
Bozanich, Pamela, 85, 86
brain function
  science of, 80
  trauma's effects on, 84–85
Brantley, Alan, 94
Brown University, 149
Bundy, Ted, 28
bureaucracy, 62
Buress, Hannibal, 148–149
burglary, 94
Burr, Aaron, 12

C
Capote, Truman, 27–28
cars
  Kemper's theft of, 187–189
  University of Idaho student
    killings and, 186–187

Carylene (Scott's victim), 95
Castor, Bruce, 146, 151, 163, 164
celebrity trials, *In Cold Blood* and, 28
change, aversion to, 203
Cheltenham Township (PA) Police
    Station, 144
child abuse
  Menendez case and, 36
  murder of parents and, 43, 70–72
choice, loss of, 206
CID (Criminal Investigation
    Command), 97
civil suit against Cosby, 146–148,
    149–150, 153
Clark, Sally, 210–211
class tensions, 109, 127–128
climate change, 216
Clutter family, 27–28
CNN, 151, 164
Colorado Supreme Court, 25
confabulation, 117–118
confidence-style rapists, 90–91,
    92, 96
confirmation bias, 86, 176, 190, 211
Constand, Andrea, 135–137, 138–144,
    146–153, 155–171, 208
Constitution, 26
Conte, Jon, 36–37, 42, 45, 87–88
Cooney, Jim, 36, 105–110, 125,
    127–130, 132
Cooper, Roy, 132
Coopers & Lybrand, 37
Cosby, Bill, 135–153, 155–171, 208
Cosby Show, The, 137
couples therapy, 199–200

trauma *(cont.)*
  effects of, 84–85, 143–144,
    151, 155, 157–158,
    163–164, 196
  evidence-based trauma assessment
    and, 193
  flashbacks and, 196–197, 200
  limbic system and, 151, 164
  memory and, 113, 123, 125, 139,
    151, 158, 164
  of rape and sexual assault, 22
  rape trauma syndrome and,
    74–75
  sensory recollections and, 157
trauma-informed approach, 122,
  155, 193
trial strategy, 70–73, 152–153
true crime
  In Cold Blood and, 27–28
  expansion of interest in, 29–30
  humanization of, 30
trust, 96, 193
truth, 1, 3, 88, 92, 121, 151, 180,
  181, 188–189, 209, 216, 217
Twitter, 151, 164

U

United States national gymnastics
  team, 192, 204
United States v. Stinson, 98
University of Idaho student killings,
  185–186
University of Pennsylvania, 137
U.S. Army Criminal Investigation
  Command (CID), 97

V

Vanity Fair, 42, 81
Vicary, William, 43
victim impact statements, 203–206
victims. *See also* false allegations;
  individual victims
  bias against, 208
  blaming of, 30–31, 91, 167
  delayed reporting and, 96
  FBI training regarding, 76
  flashbacks and, 196–197, 200
  gender bias and, 85, 87
  lack of belief and, 191
  lack of support for, 198
  memory and, 158
  in Nasser case, 203
  polygraphs and, 97–98
  preexisting beliefs regarding,
    69–70
  SANE (Sexual Assault Nurse
    Examiner) reports and,
    122–124
  support for, 32, 169, 205
  trauma and, 80–81

W

Wallace, Henry Louis, 36, 105–106
Watts, Rosalyn "Roz," 137–138
Weeks, Ezra, 11–12
Weeks, Levi, 11–12
Weinstein, Harvey, 168–169
Weisberg, Stanley M., 74, 87
Wells, England, Folkes case in, 6–11
Westbury Music Fair, 28
Williams, Alan, 210–211

About the Authors

Dr. Ann Wolbert Burgess, DNSc., APRN, is a leading forensic and psychiatric nurse who has worked with the FBI for over two decades. She is currently a professor at the Boston College Connell School of Nursing, and she lives in Boston, Massachusetts.

Steven Matthew Constantine is the associate director of marketing and communications at the Boston College Connell School of Nursing. He holds an MFA from the Bennington Writing Seminars and maintains a small orchard outside of Boston.